INFLUENCER SECRETS

A slap in your face for NOT being on Facebook LIVE every day, talking about just ONE specific topic for 90 days and NOT selling 6 to 7-figures of ONE specific product that's related to your topic... -OR- How to waste a million dollars online a year for not showing up...

INFLUENCER SECRETS

For people that have a dream to become an influencer, create a mass movement, and impact people's lives…

GENE ADAM

Copyright 2018 by Gene Adam, All Rights Reserved

No part of this book may be reproduced or transmitted in any form or by any means, electronic or mechanical, without written permission from the author, except for the use of brief quotations in a review.

First edition June 2018

Disclaimer:

While the author believes that anyone who can put in the work can achieve success using these tools, the results in this book are not typical. The author makes no claims to a guarantee of success using these methods.

Gene Adam believes that authors should be compensated for their hard work and he will absolutely get compensated for any link or referral in this book. Gene Adam not only teaches how to make money online but he gets paid from coaches, influencers, speakers, courses, affiliate programs, seminars, interviews and his books.

It's imperative that you understand how the influencer business works and how you can do the same.

CONTENTS

CONTENTS	vii
Dedication	ix
What is 7 Figure Facebook Influencer Secrets?	1
Introduction	5
Influencer Principles	9
The Promise Note	19
Moral Obligations of an Influencer	21
SECTION ONE: INFLUENCER GOLD RUSH	27
Secret #1 Why Are Influencers Getting So Rich and All the Attention?	29
Secret #2 How Do Influencers Deliver Results?	33
Secret #3 How You Can Build an Audience Without Paying For Ads	37
SECTION TWO: FIVE CORE ELEMENTS OF AN INFLUENCER	45
Secret #4 How to Build YOU as a Personal Brand	49
Secret #5 THEM: How to Find Your Perfect Audience	65
Secret #6 Find and Validate Their PROBLEM	73
Secret #7 How to Write Your STORY	79
Secret #8 How to SELL Without Selling	89
SECTION THREE: CREATING CONTENT	111
Secret #9 What Kind of Content Should You Create?	113
Secret #10 How to Come Up with Wanted Content for Facebook Lives	117
Secret #11 How to Write Effective Posts	131

SECTION FOUR: HOW TO GET TRAFFIC, UNLIMITED FOLLOWERS, FANS AND BUYERS — 137
Secret #12 How to Crush It With Facebook Groups — 139
Secret #13 Do 1 Facebook Live Every Day — 149
Secret #14 How to Show Up Everywhere - 3X Content Multiplier — 155

SECTION FIVE: CREATING YOUR FUNNEL, BONUSES AND UPSELLS — 159
Secret #15 Facebook Profile Funnel — 163

Want a Highly Converting Funnel Done-For-You for FREE? (Value:$1000) — 169
Conclusion — 173
References — 177
Want to get your own funnel? — 178

Dedication

I want to dedicate this book to my dad. It seemed like my dad always was able to solve any situation even though there was pretty much no way out.

Because of my dad I was able to move from the Ukraine to the U.S. by myself at 16 years old. With one-way ticket and with no way to come back home in mind I could integrate into the American System, go to a San Francisco school, and then go to a Silicon Valley college, stay in the U.S. and live my life I always wanted on my own terms.

A few years back my dad had a stroke and now he's getting better and better but still he's got those nasty medications which I hope he can get rid of one day… Thank you for your kindness dad!

My lovely girlfriend that supported me through the worst times. She kept on supporting me financially even though I was so broke while the whole society was laughing at her for helping me. It's funny how people look at a woman helping a broke guy financially... She saw in me something and that means a lot to me. She is definitely a high-quality woman out there...

I want to thank everybody I've been associated with. To get to this point, I went through a lot of mentors and a lot of partners. Most of my partnerships turned out to be failures but I learned a lot and I want to thank them anyway because it moved me closer to who I am today.

To my daughter Emma who given me a reason to try to make the world a better place. Your future is what drives me to take huge risks in my life.

I want to thank you, who is reading this book, reading my blog and watching my videos and Facebook lives. I am deeply indebted to all of you. You all made me grow.

* * *

So, girls and boys! Are you ready to take a leap of faith and start build your personal brand so you can make more sales and live your life on your own terms?

Let's do it together! I'll be here along the way to guide you.

What is 7 Figure Facebook Influencer Secrets?

If you are an entrepreneur you need this book like air, unless you figured the influencer game out...

First of all, let me explain what I mean by "needing this book like air". 😅

Here's what this book is about:

1. *7 Figure Facebook Influencer Secrets* will help you find <u>your voice</u> and give you <u>confidence</u> to become a <u>leader</u> in your niche.

2. *7 Figure Facebook Influencer Secrets* will help you build your audience

3. *7 Figure Facebook Influencer Secrets* will teach you how to sell without being salesy. No need to beg anyone to buy from you.

4. *7 Figure Facebook Influencer Secrets* will show you how to become more profitable and allow you to live your life on your own terms.

Who's this book for?

If you are missing any of the pieces above then this book is definitely for you.

If you are willing to take action and you are motivated then it's for you. If you:
- need to build audience
- don't want to spend money for Facebook ads
- want more engagement
- want more sales
- are stuck but don't know what to do next
- are a beginner and need to establish yourself
- are an expert in your niche but don't know how to become and influencer

- are not confident but you know deep inside that maybe you can do it
- feel that all the work you have done doesn't seem to get you where you want to be
- have a product already but you don't know how to sell it
- are a stay at home mom / dad who wants to set up a course or a membership site
- are interested in making a side income

This book is NOT for, if you:
- are satisfied were you are at and you don't have a problem to solve
- don't want to grow your audience and you already have a big established brand
- don't want to make more sales
- are not able to follow the plan
- are not going to take action or willing to do the work
- don't want to change anything
- are lazy

Introduction

FROM A $26K/MONTH TO DEAD BROKE

Life is so unpredictable if you take risks. Let's say you took a huge risk, and transferred $5000 from your account to a manufacturer's account to buy one hot product that you are pretty sure you can sell. You open an ecommerce store and it explodes. It sells day and night. One day, you are taking a vacation in Spain, money is coming in right into your bank account on autopilot and you are enjoying your life… Everything seems to be fine. You've made it! Congratulations! YES! Awesomeness. So you are sitting on the top of the world enjoying it… 😎

And then BOOM something bad happens. Like the owner of the product decides to stop selling you their product because they see how much money you make… Hm… Smells like an opportunity they thought… and so they jump on it and cut off all the distributors so they can sell it by themselves… After you spent $120,000 on advertising their product you suddenly get cut off the grid… You can't buy this product anymore and because it's patented you can't get it anywhere else. And, so obviously, your sales stop…

And so that's how your business stops. An unexpected turn cuts your income completely to ZERO and without this product your business is completely gone.

After the last cash is gone, you lose your business, savings, investment and you get into debt -$30,000… So you lose it all… You can't even pay your rent anymore… BOOM! just like that. You're homeless again. The world is not friendly anymore. So-called "friends" are gone, or were they real friends? Family looks at you like you're stupid, or something is wrong with you. Society looks at you as you don't deserve to live at all. Who cares about losers right?

Except it was the story of my life and it was so damn real, not some Hollywood movie. So, it left me depressed and dead broke.

And then one day it hit me. I just finished reading the book Crush It by Gary Vaynerchuk and I had a huge epiphany.

Wait a minute… I spent so much money on ads, I spent so much energy to build someone else's business for years and then all of my wealth was gone within a few months… This can't be right! I knew then, that somewhere along the way I've made a mistake.

It hit me. If I would build a name for myself and people would know me as a personal brand this would have never happened to me.

If I had a *Gene Adam* brand a few years back and I had 1 million followers, there's no way that all of 1 million people would unfollow me at once... But if there was the Manufacturer's name all over it – he got all the credit...

Moreover, if I had my brand, I could sell a new product to my audience again and again. And if I do it right I could continue building my personal brand turning more and more people into fans that like me, follow me and buy from me...

And so my influencer journey began. I started studying like there's no tomorrow. Sleepless nights, lots of coffee and lots of chocolate just to stay awake.

I've learned more about influencers than any course could teach me. I just kept on going to influencer profiles on Facebook and kept on looking for clues why they got so many likes, shares and followers. I started putting the puzzles together and I will share the knowledge I got in this book. Some things that influencer do are so obvious and some are not obvious at all... The good news is that anyone can repeat these steps and become an influencer in their market and start making sales effortlessly without paying for ads.

READY TO HAVE YOUR BRAIN EXPLODED?

I read a lot. I read 100 books per year… That means that every morning I wake up and educate myself just like Bill Gates, Mark Zuckerberg, Elon Musk and Warren Buffet do…

Why do you think I do that? So I can write a lot. I can never run out of ideas. Because if you read some awesome books by Tim Ferriss, Russell Brunson, Grant Cardone, Gary V, etc – your ideas will start exploding in your head… It's endless…

So, before you start reading this book you need to understand the principles that will help you become an influencer.

An Invitation

Throughout this book, you will catch references to Gene Adam's Influencer Coaching. If you're not familiar with his thriving training for entrepreneurs and the opportunities for business and personal growth it offers, please accept the invitation at:

http://geneadam.com/ic

There's no reason not to do it immediately. You need not complete this book first.

Influencer Principles

To be a very effective influencer you got to incorporate and use these principles <u>all the time</u>. If you don't use just one of them, you are risking to fail your influencer career. Every principle is a piece of a puzzle.

PRINCIPLE #1. GET VOCAL

Influencers show up on camera every single day, in other words you need to be in the public eye. If you don't show up just one day your brand plunges a notch lower. And if you don't show up for 2 or 3 months your brand can completely disappear and no one will even care if you exist. There are some exceptions if you are a big influencer, but as a rule of thumb it's true 90% of the time.

Why is it so? We live in such a fast-evolving world that it takes 60-90 days to forget about you... ouch! It hurts! I know... I'll talk more about it in later chapters.

PRINCIPLE #2. TAKE MASSIVE ACTION - AS YOUR LIFE DEPENDS ON IT

Just do the damn work. I'm so tired of seeing people talking a lot but doing little. "Taking Action" is so overrated. It's all over internet, yet almost no one takes action. 90% of people don't! See, the thing is if there's no major problem in your life that's forcing you to take action you probably won't take action. If your life seems as "it's all good", you probably won't change a thing about it... Because you won't have a need to get out of your comfort zone... Why would you? All is good, right?

But if you have a strong force, or a strong desire to change, you will take massive action.

Do you have kids? Hm... Will you do the right thing and put them in the best school you can? Will you help them to start their career when they turn 16?

Got old parents? Would you help them when they get really sick? Personally, I'm working on retiring my dad so he never has to work again especially after his stroke. And in this day and age you have to work till you drop... Some people can't afford to retire ever... 😳

I think you get my point. See "taking action" isn't some cool phrase you have to memorize and play with... But you need to realize that we are all mortal creatures that going to completely disappear within the next 100 years… And most likely no one will hear our names again…

So, if you have the last 30 days of your life starting tomorrow, what is it going to be? Are you going to watch another funny cat video on YouTube? Or are you going to make some changes in your life and help some people around you?

And if you are completely alone and you have absolutely no family, would you like to change it all? With your career success you can become successful in other areas… personal life, health, and spiritual side. Because it almost always goes hand in hand. Just got to get your puzzles together…

"Taking action" is a force, it's a kick in the butt… Use it in your advantage. Find out what pisses you off the most right now… Take that energy and turn it into fruits… Got lemons? Make yourself a lemonade and don't forget some ice and a straw…

PRINCIPLE #3. BE SCARED BUT DO IT ANYWAY. HAVE YOUR WHY BIGGER THAN YOUR FEARS.

People are scared of cameras and being on stage. And it's totally normal I get it. We are wired this way. "I'll never be on camera", "I'll never come on stage, I hate it". "There's no way I want to be in a public eye, it's just not me". I hear this A LOT!

Well it really depends if you never will be on camera or maybe you will…

If you had no choice, and this was your last chance to survive about 100% of you would do anything. It's really about how bad you want it and that's all it is...

If you were hanging on the cord under a bridge that just broke off below the Mount Everest, and all you see is abyss all around you, and someone came up to you and asked you, "Hey, want to get on a Facebook Live with me if I help you?", I don't think your first answer will be "I hate being on videos"... Your first answer will be "I'll do anything, just please get me out of here".

So suddenly you just turned into "I'll-do-anything" mentality and your WHY just shifted.

Hm.. 🤐 Really? Just now? 😁

How do I know? Because I'm wired exactly the same way as any human walking on this planet Earth. And second, I was just like that not too long ago. Something had to push me so hard and give me such a huge kick in the butt, that I couldn't remember my name. 😱

Let me ask you this, would you prefer living a mediocre life without taking any risks or would you like to take a leap of faith and make a change that could possibly give you a better life?

Taking a risk is almost like a "jumping-off-cliff" mentality, we all fear it but it could be hugely rewarding.

Getting out of comfort zone creates the most amazing things in life. It can fly you to the moon, paint like Picasso, or play on stage like Elvis Presley...

Elvis Presley once said, "The first time that I appeared on stage, it scared me to death."

There's a great book called *Feel The Fear and Do it Anyway* by Susan Jeffreys where she says, I don't know where in my life I would be now if I didn't take risks...

You have two choices: Embrace uncertainty or stay mediocre.

PRINCIPLE #4. GIVE AWAY SO MUCH VALUE THEY CAN'T IGNORE YOU!

Scarcity just doesn't work! The reason many of my partnerships failed was because my partners almost always wanted to charge money first. And once I realized this, I broke those partnerships. And, guess what? They are still trying to sell their products without giving anything to anyone. Zero value. Who wants that crap. No wonder that most of them are still struggling.

You see, it's not just in the Bible, that you shall give and you shall receive, it's our human nature.

What if you did exactly the opposite of what everyone else is doing? Try it sometime. What separates big influencers from small ones is how much value they give away for free.

Tai Lopez is giving away cars. Grant Cardone is giving away 1 million dollars on Facebook, Twitter and Instagram.

Yes, the price tags of their giveaways are huge and unreal for most of us. I agree, but the value isn't only in the money and cars. When you become a mega influencer, you can sure do that too, but it's not necessary.

We can give HUGE VALUE by simply giving awesome information away. You can give away courses, books, software, checklists, infographics, videos, etc. for absolutely free and build your following on Facebook fast!

Give first and don't wait until you receive anything. Keep on going. Give more. Give out your best stuff. Make them wonder and think: "If your free stuff is so damn good, I wonder what quality the paid stuff will be…". When you give anything, engage with them. Make them like, share, comment, follow you on FB, make them join your Facebook Group. etc. Giving your stuff away doesn't mean getting rid of your stuff for nothing. It means giving your stuff to build your personal brand.

PRINCIPLE #5. ALWAYS BE SELLING

I don't mean to say every 5 minutes "buy my stuff", "buy my stuff"… NO! that's not how to do this right. And I don't mean to spam your links on your wall, in Facebook Groups and Messenger either. That's not how you sell.

What I mean by always be selling is structure your free content the way that it effortlessly sells your paid stuff. Sometimes you don't even have to sell it hard at all. If your offer is sexy it can sell on its own by mentioning it once or twice. That said, you have to be very confident and firm when you ask for the sale. Just as a doctor would say, "Take 1 pill in the morning and 1 pill in the evening, now, go downstairs and buy the pills there". See, it can be casual but it's a command. I will talk about this in later chapters.

Also, have your offer (paid offer) always ready. Many of my students create amazing content, but they don't have anything to sell yet.

That means that if you do have a lot of free content already, you need to be ready to offer something that people can buy. Otherwise you won't make any money.

As a rule of thumb, you should have 90% free value content and 10% pitching.

You can simply introduce a paid offer by mentioning it in the end of your FB lives, but there are even better ways to do it which I will mention in the coming chapters.

PRINCIPLE #6. STAY CONSISTENT

Show up in front of people's eyes every single day, non-stop. Do daily Facebook lives. You can add daily Instagram lives and Youtube lives, but in the beginning just pick one platform and go with it all the way. Stay consistent and don't stop. In 60-90 days, people will almost completely forget about you. If you stop today, all of your work you have done previously would be a waste!

By the way, you can use other platforms, it doesn't have to be Facebook, but pick the platform that will allow you to be in front of people right away. If you do daily blogs, for example, your site has to be ranked high on search engines in order for people to read your blogs. And if you got 0 people visiting your blog, that might be a flop.

So, look for the platform that can INSTANTLY show your face in front of people and do it consistently every single day.

PRINCIPLE #7. CONCENTRATE

Stop all distractions. It sounds too simple except that it's not. If you filmed yourself for one day you would be surprised how much time you waste every day on stuff that isn't important.

Do you listen to music in the car? I rarely do. Why? Because <u>my life depends on it</u>. So, I listen to an audio book.

Do you watch a 1-hour videos on YouTube (like comedy, music vids, not business related tutorials) that's kinda, sorta interesting, but probably it will not help you in your business? I stop myself from doing that. <u>My life depends on it</u>. I need to finish writing this book.

Do you like eating long lunches with your girlfriends / buddies every single day? I don't. I used to, but <u>my life depends on it</u>. By the way, I do have friends that share my interests, but having a long talk for 2-3 hours about non-business related things is a time killer. That's a 2-3 hour of writing right there. If you are a big party girl/guy, limit it to a few evenings per week and only when your brain is tired anyway.

* * *

That's it! Those are the 7 principles you need to master today.

It's easier to follow these principles if your life depends on it, but if you are comfortable where you are now, you simply won't take action.

If the force is not strong enough you simply won't do it.

Ok, so I don't like to beat around the bush and I don't like fluff...

Here's what we are going to do. I want you to sign the Promise Note to yourself that declares that you will do what it takes to be an influencer.

The Promise Note

Before you read any further. Print this promise note to yourself. Sign it. And leave it on your desk. Download the PDF promise note here: www.geneadam.com/promise-note.pdf

- Everything I read in Influencer Secrets book is super easy to implement.

- If I just use these steps laid out in the book I can get more followers and exposure like influencers do.

- I will get VOCAL at least once a day and make at least 1 Facebook Live about a topic related to my niche.

- I will take massive ACTION because my life and many other lives depend on it.
- I will get out of my comfort zone because my WHY is bigger than my FEARS of being on camera and being in the public eye!

- I will give away so much VALUE that they can't ignore me.

- I will have my OFFER ready so I can start selling and making money with my brand!

- I will stay CONSISTENT and will show up every day on Facebook Lives because my life depends on it.

- I will CONCENTRATE on my business and stop doing unimportant, distracting things in my life that suck my time and energy which keep me away from my success

- I will EDUCATE myself with important information about my business so I become a better and smarter version of myself. (books, courses, seminars, etc.)

- If I find a golden nugget I will stop reading and IMPLEMENT the new ideas right away.

- Nothing will stop me. I will implement this plan and I will SUCCEED!

_____ (Your Name)

_____ (Today's Date)

Moral Obligations of an Influencer

So, let's say you are a BIG star. You are an influencer already. You are worth $100,000,000...

What's next BOSS? Your life is about to get very boring... You got what you wanted, you travelled all over the globe, your bought cars and houses, ate amazing food and you found the love of your life, paid Elon Musk $5,000,000 to travel to the moon or whatever you imagined to achieve, and now what?

Why wait until you become somebody? Money likes speed. Money attracts winners. Winners attract money. The winner take it all. All the way home. The sooner you start behaving like a winner the faster you will become a winner. The true winners give back. The stingy disappear in history.

The next obvious step for many rich people is to give a huge portion of their wealth away.

Good deeds, giving, helping, donating and making the world a better place seems to be the next level for anyone's success.

MORAL OBLIGATION #1. GIVE

If you want to show results, there's a nice formula you might have heard of, "Give and you shall receive". Some say this formula is about 2000 years old. But, it's probably more like 4000 years old if not older. Either way, the point is, it's still working today and it ain't going to stop working anytime soon.

Just go and find somebody you can work for free and then get some results and ask if they would give you a testimonial.

Another thing you can do is shoot Facebook lives with the most amazing content you possess. Just give it away. People will be psyched.

"If she gives away this stuff for free, wow, what does she have in store for me when I want to pay for her services?"

"If he's giving me this awesome content for free, I wonder what's his paid stuff look like?"

MORAL OBLIGATION #2. BE SINCERE AND HONEST

Be a good one. Don't be a bad influencer. Don't be a show off. Don't pretend you are better than you really are. People smell it from far, far away. Just be yourself. Don't tell people you make a lot of money if you don't. The truth always prevails. It's all about being true to yourself and others.

So, what do you do if you don't make a lot of money but you are just starting? Tell them you are <u>on your journey to figure out X</u>. Tell them, "<u>I will teach you how to get [amazing desired results] without [the biggest pain]</u>", and then go and teach it for free. Examples: "How to fly an airplane in 1 week without studying a 5-year flight school", "How to play a guitar in 2 hours without taking any music lessons". When you make a bold promise, always deliver it.

MORAL OBLIGATION #3. DON'T FAKE IT TILL YOU MAKE IT

There are a lot of guru that say you can fake it till you make it. So should you do it?

I know you are eager to start making money quick, but if you "fake it" you might be shooting yourself in the foot.

There are times when you CAN "fake it till you make it".

Fake it internally. Don't fake it externally.

You CAN "fake it" for motivation, for example:

- I feel great,
- I know I can do it,
- I'm the man,
- I'm the super woman... Past
- etc.

You can tell stories to yourself internally, you can be somebody and you can become it. It works.

Almost everything I ever wanted in my life happened to me, because I programmed myself and told myself in present tense that I already have it. It's your moral obligation to make yourself grow.

That said, you CAN'T "fake it" externally by telling people that you are somebody you are not. You can't fake your results. Don't fake it. It won't work. Don't pretend. People will know. It's your moral obligation not to lie and pretend.

MORAL OBLIGATION #4. SELL THEM YOUR PRODUCTS FOR THEIR OWN GOOD

One of my earlier mentors, Jay Abraham, kept on repeating that it's my moral obligation to sell what's good for my customers. And I just couldn't get the gist of it. It seemed so strange to me somehow. I felt bad about selling my stuff, asking for money and then telling myself it's my obligation. How can it be an obligation when I take their money and put it in my pocket?

But after he repeated it 3 times, I started getting it.

It's "your obligation" when your product will change your customer's life, solve their problem or increase their status. Of course, it also implies that your product is awesome and you genuinely believe it will help them. Your offer has to be so good that they gotta be crazy not to take this offer.

> "If you truly believe that what you have is useful and valuable to your clients, then you have a moral obligation to try and serve them in every way possible." — Jay Abraham

If your product is so good and you truly believe that it will help your customer you MUST sell it to them and it's your moral obligation!

MORAL OBLIGATION #5. DONATE MONEY AND HELP THE ONES IN NEED

After all of your successes what else is left for you to do? Give back... That sounds great, but what if you haven't made money yet?

To start donating you should start giving money away when you are poor. That's right, you are training your brain to give when you don't have much and you will continue giving away when you are rich. Take 10-30% off your salary and give it away. I guarantee what you give you will get back tenfold.

Did you make $1000 last month? Give away $100... you made $1 Mil? Give away, $100,000.

It's always proportionate to what you make, so don't be scared. If you make only $10, give $1.

It always comes back! It works!

Many years ago, one of my mentors told me that if I don't start donating money when I am poor, I'm unlikely to become rich.

I said, why?

He said, it's an abundance exercise. When you give money away, you are not attached to money and you are not scared to lose it. It's about knowing that you can get it back. It's about knowing that if you take a risk with a high potential you'll get your money back.

So, what are you passionate about? What are you angry about that you would like to change? What can make this world a better place? Does it have a charity?

As I'm writing this book, I'm donating to my dream charity called *The Ocean Cleanup* @ www.theoceancleanup.com

I got so angry about the islands of plastic garbage in the ocean, I still can't understand why people use so much plastic in the world, even though it's not really needed.

Here's an excerpt of my charity:

"Over 5 trillion pieces of plastic currently litter the ocean. Trash accumulates in 5 ocean garbage patches, the largest one being the Great Pacific Garbage Patch, located between Hawaii and California. If left to circulate, the plastic will impact our ecosystems, health and economies. Solving it requires a combination of closing the source, and cleaning up what has already accumulated in the ocean."

I feel so terribly bad about this and our planet Earth, and I'd like to be involved in a project to help our planet on a larger scale.

How do you really feel? What footprint would you leave in 100 years from now when you are gone?

SECTION ONE:
INFLUENCER GOLD RUSH

So gold rush repeats again and again. There are new industries born and gone just like supernovas. Some industries stay for 100s years or longer some not. This one for sure is a strange one.

In 1900s we got a trend of famous singers, dancers, movie stars...

In 2000s it started shifting toward individual talent of you and I right from the comfort of our homes. YouTube created homemade stars that never had a chance to become famous in the old world.

Not only we can be super visible now but also newly made influencers can get VERY,VERY RICH just by showing up every day and growing their audiences to millions of people just like famous movie stars.

The new currency of this century is the attention of your responsive audience, who are also your fans that can buy from you again and again.

The funny thing is that the REAL stars (singers, actors) now hire influencers to help them to get their word out.

So technically it's more advantageous to be an influencer today than a Rockstar 50-100 years ago…

"Yeah, but, but… I'm not an expert…" That's a very false statement. Don't listen to your little inner voice when it says that. Anyone can be an expert as long as they know just a little tiny bit more than the person next to them. I'll cover this in the coming chapters.

One thing I want you to be sure about that anyone can do it. You don't need a special talent to be an influencer. All you need is a special skill which I will go over in the book.

You can do this!

It would be awesome if I could remind you to be awesome and write this sentence on a sticky note and put it next to your computer:

"I got this. I can do it!"

Do it now or you will forget to do it later. By the way, I have this note on my computer too. ;)

Secret #1
Why Are Influencers Getting So Rich and All the Attention?

So you might wonder what's all the fuss about?

Well, frankly, if you are an influencer you are like Coca Cola or McDonalds except you are a person. It's a new title that has not existed just 10 years ago. Or at least the word didn't have the same meaning.

Becoming an "influencer" means a lot in 2020s, if you got thousands of followers. One thing is for sure it's not going away anytime soon.

If you got 2000 active members in your FB group it could make you $20,000 a month.

Example: if you only sell a $500 course (or any other product) you only need to sell 40 people in your Facebook Group to get to $20K/month. So having only a few thousand people will do.

But that's still a very small game... 20K/month is not even a million a year...

Let me make an example what Tai Lopez can pull with his numbers. He's got around 6 million people on his Facebook Page... When he speaks on a Facebook Live he gets sometimes 500-1000 likes per post on a slow day... And Facebook is only one of many platforms he uses. As a side note, one of his YouTube videos got about 70 million views which leads a potential customer to a sale.

He sells courses successfully... He is also a co-owner of a multi-million dollar business called Mentor Box. And he also owns a very successful business with Sam Ovens. Sam Ovens has sold over $20 Million in courses...

Grant Cardone? The same. He wrote more than 5 books and he's made most of his money in Real Estate. He definitely does his influencer marketing non-stop even though he's worth over 500 million dollars already. So you might ask why being an influencer is so beneficial to Grant Cardone?

The truth is being an influencer Grant has found real estate deals, investors, partners, buyers and his true fans. He sold an unbelievable amount of books because of his publicity.

Gary Vaynerchuk? The same. Sold gazillion books. One of the classics you might have heard of "Crush it" which is one of the first books that talked about the influencer revolution that's coming... that was published back in 2009... Wow. It was written over 10 years ago.

So what are they worth?

Gary Vaynerchuk: 160 million

Grant Cardone: over 500 million
Tony Robbins: over 500 million
and so on…

But don't get discouraged by the big numbers. That was not my point. My point is you can grow your audience exponentially and succeed as an influencer.

Look, in 2020s YOU MUST BECOME AN INFLUENCER. If you don't do it now, you already lost the game! If you don't do it someone else will establish their name in your industry. You see younger generation doesn't have a "pause" button. They are already here. Let them just graduate from high-school and the opportunity is gone. They are born with it.

Let's take somebody smaller like Josh Forti. He got only a little over 14,000 followers on his personal Facebook as of writing this book. He's a 20 something guy. He sold his course. He's millionaire already.

So this secret is all about making you realize that you there's no way out. If you want to become successful today, you need to become an influencer.

Influencers are rock stars of our generation. They get at all the attention because they show up all over the internet whether it's posts, photos, videos, lives, ads, blogs, webinars or podcasts. They are just about anywhere where it is humanly possible to show up in any form.

Here's a quick note to non-believers.

Tai Lopez lived in a mobile home in the middle of nowhere with $47 on his bank account just a few years ago.

Grant Cardone used to be a drug addict. He almost died. He was almost homeless. Didn't pay rent for 3 months asking his landlord to stay a little longer.

Tony Robbins left his home at 17 away from his alcoholic abusive mother, slept in the car for months.

I personally have been homeless twice in my life. Once when I came to America and the other time when I made it and lost it all.

Please, please believe me, almost ALL influencers started from NOTHING. There's a 1% percent exception to this rule. But I don't even know the names of the gold spoon influencers that inherited this from their Mommy or Daddy. Maybe Bushes? Or the English Queen? 😊

The rest of us mortals started from absolutely zero and we have a BIG reason WHY we want to do it that drives us to become a better version of ourselves.

Secret #2
How Do Influencers Deliver Results?

Easy. They Create personas. Build audiences. Show up everywhere. Create a lot of VALUE in the niche. Give it away for FREE. Create offers. Get attention. Sell their products. That's about it. That was the short version. 😊

Now the longer version.

They make their Facebook wall/page look like a very attractive place for people to visit. Just like a nicely designed restaurant with awesome ambience and amazing food.

They do Facebook Live videos every single day. The reason they do Facebook Lives is because it beats the Facebook algorithm and they show up on top.

And then, they do the same thing on Instagram, Youtube, Twitter, or ANY hot platform that is waiting us around the corner in the year 2020, 2030, 2040, etc…

They teach people a lot of amazing and wanted content what people crave for.

Influencers create the type of content that gets attention.

They create great offers.

And only once in a long while they sell… 90% great content / 10% pitching is a good rule of thumb.

Influencers sell just about anything… Courses, coaching, 1-on-1, video trainings, webinars, books, seminars and almost any type of services and products. They also have the best connections in the industry. They can partner and collaborate on projects. They are invited to podcasts, interviews and other Facebook Lives. And by building their personal brand they become even bigger.

Sounds quite simple! Except it's not. I'll go over details in the later chapters…

And one more interesting thing what influencers do. They create ecosystems. They show up everywhere they can with their stuff.

You can just spy on the biggest whales and you'll see what they are doing. If you check Grant Cardone, Gary Vaynerchuk, Tai Lopez, you will see how they show up everywhere.

For example, influencer ecosystem can look like this:

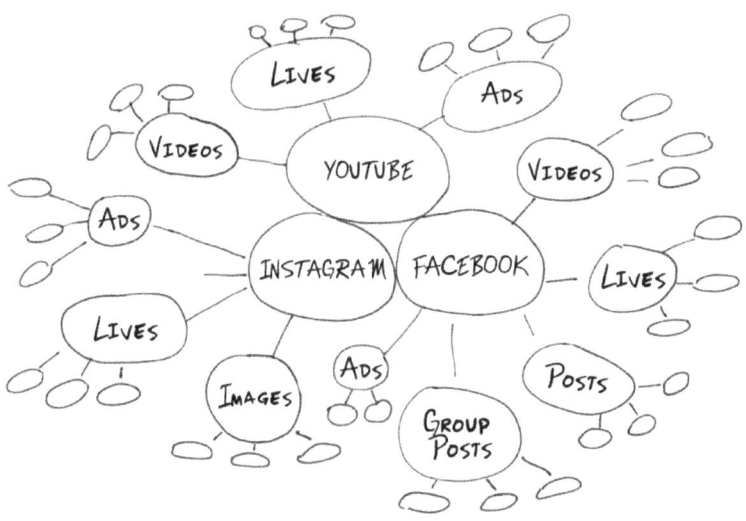

So, let's say the influencer is on these 3 BIG platforms: Facebook, YouTube and Instagram. If you look at the diagram how they show up everywhere by posting content every single day, then you'll see what I mean.

Now, I didn't mention the other things they do like Podcasts and JV Partnerships. They leverage other people's audiences to get bigger and BIGGER! It's endless.

In this book I will cover mostly the Facebook part but I want you to see the big picture. Eventually, your goal should be to show up on every possible platform. That said, don't confuse yourself with too many platforms at the moment. Pick one and go with that one all the way and later you can always do more.

Just remember, you can leverage other people's audiences and use it to grow your network exponentially.

I will use Facebook platform in this book a lot, because it's the biggest, but later don't forget to develop ecosystems and show up on multiple platforms.

Secret #3
How You Can Build an Audience Without Paying For Ads

Influencers grow HUGE audiences fast. So right off the bat, let's talk about how you can do that.

There is a way you can implement right away to get unlimited audience without paying for ads.

ONE TO MANY

Always find a way to present your material to masses and talk "one-to-many". What is "one-to-many"? When you call ONE of your friends or chat to ONE client at a time, that's "one-to-one". When you talk to MANY people at once you talk "one-to-many".

Whether you have a podcast and you talk with your voice once and dozens of people listen, or it's a YouTube video that you recorded once and it's got hundreds of people watching, or it's a blog that you wrote once and many people read it, it's all "one-to-many".

Here are a few "one-to-many" ideas you could implement right now:
- Host Facebook lives
- Create videos on YouTube
- Write Facebook posts
- Document your life on Instagram
- Write blog posts
- Get on TV / news online
- Show up on any media platform where crowds of people reside.

What is the difference between paying for an ad and having a "one-to-many" strategy? Nothing... Except that you have to pay for ads and go broke doing that. (Unless you make 6-7 figures already, you don't need to pay for ads).

The good news is that the "one-to-many" strategy is free but you have to show up every day for the next 90-180 days doing one thing and one thing only.

If you choose to do Facebook lives, go all in, and do Facebook lives only, not 100 other things you could be doing on other different platforms.

Do it for the next 90 days non-stop. It doesn't matter what media you choose to show up on.

Neil Patel wrote his blog posts every day for 1 year and he became a blog expert just by doing that one type of media!

iJustine became a famous YouTuber by showing up on YouTube for many years, even though she produced funny silly videos that were unrelated to any market!

Pat Flynn showed up on his podcast for one year and became a famous podcaster!

> The next influencer could be you!

Now, you say, ok that sound good, I will pick one media platform and go for it, but what if no one will watch my videos? After all, no one knows me?

Yes! That's a great question to ask. Everyone who's a success today started one day, right? And most of them had no fans at all.

So, here's what will happen. The first video you'll post, no one will show up. Period. It's totally normal. Ok, maybe your mom will show up. In fact, the first 20-50 videos almost nobody will watch...

There are a couple of things that will happen at this early stage:
1. You'll start finding your voice (the way you speak and present information)
2. The people will slowly start following you. Yes, I said slowly. And that's a norm.

3. You will start getting better at making videos and you'll become more natural.
4. You will start caring less about the fear of rejection. You will stop worrying if people judge you or not. Sooner or later you'll start realizing that you are who you are and they have to accept you. You don't need a psychotherapist, you need more practice to get better at videos.

In the later stages you will become better and better and eventually you will be so good that you will attract people when you speak. Build the momentum and it will explode like a snowball effect.

JOIN THEM TO YOUR FACEBOOK GROUP

This secret isn't just another hack. This secret is tricky. ;) Because it's meta. I teach my students to create their own Facebook group and grow their audience by asking their potential customers to join their FB group.

So why do we want to grow your Facebook group? Because later you can convert them into buyers. It's like having your own email list of 10,000 people. And if you have laser targeted subscribers on your list, you can sell them anything anytime.

Just imagine this. You can talk and engage with them. Become friends. You can ask them anything you want. For example, you can ask them what their problems are and what you can do for to solve their problems. And then, boom! You can create a course based on their answers. You can close high-ticket clients right in your group. Do you see power in this?

There's one "but" though. You have to show up on Facebook lives, deliver massive value, make relevant posts and really engage with them. The good news is that you can work as little as 1 hour per day engaging in your group and still have amazing results. Later I will go over more about how to build a group but this is one of the easiest ways so far to create a big audience and become a 6 or 7-figure earner in the shortest time possible.

Here's a 5-step formula called **The 7-Figure Facebook Group Method** and here how it works:

1. Create a group.
2. Pick a hot niche that pays well.
3. Ask people what their biggest problem is. They'll say X.
4. Ask them 2nd time, what is your biggest struggle about X?
5. Give it to them. Create the course exactly in the words they already described it to you.

So now, I want you to create a group too. And when you talk on a Facebook LIVE on your personal timeline, ask people to join to your Facebook group.

WHY HAVING A FACEBOOK GROUP IS BETTER THAN YOUR PERSONAL PROFILE OR PAGES

You could really do the same thing on your Facebook personal profile but your personal profile has a limit of only 5,000 friends. So, having a Facebook Group is a great solution since you can have unlimited number of members.

Facebook Pages got unlimited members as well, but they lack human interaction and engagement and they are used for huge mega influencers so I would choose Facebook Groups almost every time. (until FB algorithm changes)

When you see mega influencers like Grant Cardone, Thai Lopez and others using Facebook Pages, they use them almost as their own personal profiles. Don't confuse those with Facebook Groups.

Facebook Personal Profiles could be converted into Facebook Pages, but you should do it only when you become a mega influencer. When you are just starting it will work great, because you need more human interaction and you need to show up on other people's profiles with your Facebook lives without spending thousands of dollars on ads.

WANT TO SEE MY FACEBOOK GROUP IN ACTION?

Now this is where it gets "meta". If you are not a part of my Facebook group "Influencer Builder Group", I want you to go to the URL below and join my group and ask questions about influencers and influencer marketing. You can ask anything related to the topic.

My Facebook group URL is here:
www.geneadam.com/group

See what I did there? I asked you to join my group. And this is an example of how you should do it too. You can do this by guiding your potential customers to your Facebook group from your personal profile, cover photo, your image posts, Facebook lives, and long text posts right from your wall. You can also post posts packed with value in other similar Facebook groups and teach people something. Engage and people will naturally want to become friends with you. People simply will come to check your profile because you are awesome and interesting and they probably want to find out what else you have to say. I will cover this in later chapters.

When you become friends with your potential customer, you goal is to give them a lot of free stuff, provide amazing VALUE for free that people would even pay for. In your awesome free content mention that you have a group and if they want to be a part of it, they can join.

Once they are in the group, lead the group, teach them, laugh with them, cry with them, talk to them, continue being friends with them. Engage. Daily Facebook lives can do the trick.

If you have any questions ask me in the *Influencer Builder* Group. Take your time and look what has been happening in the group. What's priceless is that you can communicate with people just like YOU and learn from each other!

Go through some videos and let me know about what your biggest struggle is when it comes to being an influencer.

SECTION TWO:
FIVE CORE ELEMENTS OF AN INFLUENCER

Before I get into the nitty and gritty. Let me show you the bird eye view of the 5 core influencer elements every influencer got.

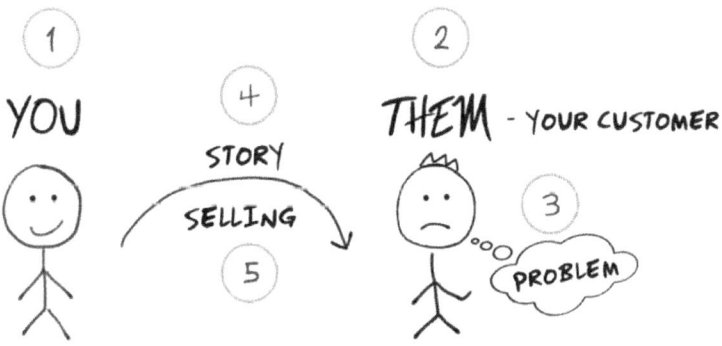

There are 5 elements:
1. YOU
2. THEM (your audience / your customer)
3. Find and validate their PROBLEM (ask them)
4. STORY (what story you are telling them)
5. SELLING

So let's go over it in more detail.

#1. You have to position YOU as an authority in your niche. You have to show up and talk to your audience as a guide.

#2. You need THEM – your perfect audience. Without audience influencers can't exist.

#3. You have to find your customer's PROBLEM.
So, if you just create a product without asking and validating your idea, most likely you won't make any money.

#4. Influencers tell STORIES all the time. That's why people like watching interesting videos of influencers if they are good storytellers. Another thing they do is they break audience's false beliefs and they replace their beliefs with something better. (use it only for good, don't use this for evil)

#5. Great influencers don't have to sell hard. They sell without selling. They incorporate stories inside of the content. They create no-brainer offers. In fact, they create such great offers that you can't help yourself but buy it.

So why are the 5 elements so crucial and why do they have to be done in this order?

Most of the time, the reason you are not making sales is not because you have a bad course, a bad video, or bad content... But because, you don't have <u>the right eyeballs</u>. (your audience).

If you got eyeballs, then you probably don't know what <u>their problem</u> is. If you know what the problem is then you probably don't tell them <u>the right story</u>. And if you got all of the above, then you don't have <u>the right offer</u>.

Here are the top 5 reasons why you don't make sales:

#1 You don't look trustworthy
#2 You don't have the right audience
#3 You don't know their problems and needs
#4 You are telling them a wrong story
#5 You don't have a great no-brainer offer to sell

Notice you have "YOU" in each of the reasons. You have "THEM" as your audience in #2. You have PROBLEMS in #3. You have a STORY in #4. And a great selling offer in #5.

If you got these 5 elements right you are very close to your goal. All you have left to do is to produce a bunch of niche related interesting content filled with value about WHY they need your product and sell them the HOW.

Sell them on WHY, deliver the HOW.

Show up in front of them and deliver. Create awesome needed stuff and they can't ignore you. We'll cover it later.

So, let's break it down into pieces in the coming secrets.

Secret #4
How to Build YOU as a Personal Brand

COURAGE

Well, first of all, you need COURAGE. It will be hard and disappointing in the beginning and you need the strength to carry on when no people show up to see you. That means you will have to work for free when you start. Wait, you say, work for free? Why didn't you tell me this earlier? 😊

Look, it is a process. It will happen but it will take a while. If you know how to control yourself and have some patience initially, you will be fine. But here's the hard truth, 1000 people just won't show up and like your videos out of nowhere and join your group. Nope. That's not how it works.

But here's the good news. 1 person will show up. Then 2. Then 3. Then 5. Then 10. Then 100. Then 1000 and so on…

It might take 100 Facebook Lives until you get any traction at all… It was true for me, and I've asked dozens of influencers, almost everyone had to go through this. This is probably the toughest part.

BIG WHY

Next you need a BIG WHY… Your why need to be soooo huge that you won't have any fear.

You have to overcome the fear of:
- video camera
- being recorded
- being in the public eye
- people judging you and saying nasty things

Some of my students are scared of the camera, some not. Some can't handle being in the public eye and some can't stand being judged.

However, these things are easy to overcome under one circumstance. Your WHY should be BIGGER than your FEARS.

You see the problem is this. If there's a force that is so strong that you would do anything, you fears won't stop you from getting it.

For example, my dad, had a stroke a few years ago. My WHY to help him was so large that even if I liked to go out for a drink at night and have a nice conversation with my best friends over lunches, that had to stop. Because my responsibility to help my dad became bigger than hanging out with other people. This is my WHY.

Another example, my daughter wasn't growing up with me under the same roof, moreover she has never visited me in my house after a nasty divorce. Not only I lost all my money because of my divorce but I couldn't see my daughter much because the court decided that way. But if I had money to pay for my lawyers I could fight to see her more because I love her. (By the way, as a side note, as I'm writing this I finally WILL see my daughter in two days from now.) This is my WHY.

And one last example. I used to be worth 1 million dollars in 2000s and I lost it all. Divorce. Depression. The feeling of misery after I hit a high point in my 20's left me tumbling into the lowest and the darkest point in my life. Homeless. Penniless. Actually, penniless would be ok, but the negative - $30,000 in debt was way worse… But that's just me.

What about you? You need to figure out YOUR why. There's no other easy way… What is it that bothers you when you are going to sleep at night? Do you have family? Kids? Do you hate your boss? What are you pissed off about the most right now? Whatever it is write your WHY down, print it out, and put it on your desk so you can look at it every day. It will remind you why you started this journey. This way when you have your why figured out you can effortlessly show up as an influencer every single day and be in front of people without fears and without second thoughts whether you are doing the right thing or not…

POSITION YOURSELF AS AUTHORITY

The quickest way to become an authority is to simply start teaching people. If you don't think you are an expert. You are. You just have to know a little more than most people know.

It's very easy to do. Open up Youtube.com and type in almost anything and you will see people answering questions and showing the know-how.

In the book *Catch Me If You Can*, Frank Abagnale tells a story about how he was an impersonator. Once he pretended he was a teacher. He says, "I wasn't qualified to teach the class, but I taught it for one semester!". And guess what? No one found out. So the FBI agent asked so how did you do it? He said, I just read 1 chapter ahead of everybody else and I could teach the class". I don't want you to pretend like Frank. I want you to be ethical and always say the truth. But, I want you to realize that you know enough to be an expert and an authority.

WORKING FOR FREE

Even though it's hard to admit, but no one wants to work for free. If you think that way, I understand. But before I let you off the hook, I need to tell you something.

> No one will pay you money until you create some value.

It hurts to hear it, but here you have it. Let me tell you a story maybe it will remind you of something.

* * *

A couple of thousand years ago, in a small city of Babylon, a poor man Arkad was sitting on the bench wrapped deep in his thoughts. He held his head in his hands and murmured to himself, "I'll never get out of this." All he was trying to do is to make enough money so he could survive in the cruel world that was around him. He had a dream to have a purse full of gold that would be his one day. Even though he didn't have any special skills, one skill Arkad possessed was creating value.

When he was younger he learned how to carve clay tablets. And he knew this… if he would carve enough clay tablets, he could have a business and people would pay a lot of gold to get those tablets done. But first he had to buy the clay tablets and spend many months to carve them and one day somebody will come and buy these tablets from him. So he decided to try it. "What else can I lose? Only my time, I guess", he again murmured to himself…

The next day, Arkad went to the clay shop and bought all the clay tablets he could find. He spent every penny he had, just to realize that there's no turning back. He had to go all in.

He spent 6 months of sleepless nights to carve them. Some days he worked without food. Luckily, his wife had a goat and he was able to survive on milk and cheese.

Then, one day, the perfect client showed up in his shop. Arkad was happy to see him. His client bought most of those clay tablets and Arkad made a pot of gold.

* * *

So Arkad delivered value first, he invested in clay tablets and carved them for 6 months first. And only then… after all the hard work, he was able to reap the rewards.

Today, you still have to do the same. You have to do the work first, create the posts and the content. There's no way around it. Embrace it and get down to work. Get results. Document your wins. Make case studies of other people you have helped.

A lot of people come to me and say, I will never work for free. Well that's why they are where they are.

I wrote 3 books, created 4 courses, built email lists, podcasts, webinars, funnels, before anything significant happened.

I took a risk and I learned a lot. I was lucky to learn from the best mentors in the world and rub shoulders with some amazing people and that shaped me to who I am today. And by the way, I'm writing this book totally on my own terms without expecting getting paid right away. It might make it, it might not, but I'll give you so much value that you can't ignore me! ☺

GIVE MASSIVE VALUE

Give so much value that they can't ignore you. Here's the truth. The more time you spend on creating quality content, the higher people will think of you. It's not about scribbling something quick and dirty and spamming the whole internet with your junk.

Here's what I did. I started learning from the best and made a lot of notes. After I found some eye-opening material I started teaching it by creating videos and courses.

So how can you learn a lot of awesome information?

Here are the steps of how I started to create massive value:

Step 1. First, I started listening to YouTube videos and podcasts for absolutely free.

Step 2. Then, I started buying physical books and audiobooks to learn some more awesome stuff.

Step 3. Then, I started paying for courses and learned even more awesome stuff.

Step 4. Then, I got a real mentor and learned the secrets in my niche to help me grow.

Spend some time. Give it some thought. Learn from the best, but be YOUR unique SELF.

Now, on the flip side I don't want you to spend too much time creating your content because you still need to move, you still have to have speed. I don't want you to spend the next 30 years writing content or writing books. You need to get a great idea and roll with it. Complete it 80-90% and click "publish".

So in short, **give massive value and do it quick!**

YOU BE YOU

There are a lot of people that want to be somebody else. But the best that can sell you is YOU.

You don't need to copy Russell Brunson, Robert Kiyosaki or Grant Cardone. You'll never be better than they are, because you are in the direct competition with their real persona. But you know what's cool? They can't be you. Even if they try, they will fail.

There is only one of you in the world. No one can be you. Only YOU can be YOU! So, Be YOU!

TELL STORIES AND BREAK FALSE BELIEFS

Next, when you give away FREE value via Facebook Lives tell stories and break your customer's FALSE BELIEFS.

Ok this one seems simple enough, but here's the thing. Facebook Lives are different from course videos.

It's not about teaching a class like a course or something. It is similar but not the same. When you do Facebook lives, you just have to break your customer's "false beliefs", while delivering value. You can teach some secrets but always introduce some elements of false beliefs they might have and break them.

> Find something they "believe in" that you know is far away from the truth and teach them why it isn't so.

In other words, find a phony story they are telling themselves and teach them the new story that will transform their old beliefs and create new beliefs that are better and can help them to achieve huge results. It's kind of like an AHA story or a transformational story, when they will say something like, "Oh, now I get it"…

Why do you need to do that? Because people find reasons why [whatever you sell] wouldn't work. That's why people don't buy from you right away and some would never buy from you at all.

Let me make a small example of a story what people believe in but is not necessarily true.

* * *

Why NOT going to college is a smarter option for a high-school graduate who wants to be a successful entrepreneur...

Well, if you want to be a successful business person you don't need to go to college. You can do this on your own. Because successful people like Michael Dell, Steve Jobs, Bill Gates and Mark Zuckerberg, they all are college dropouts. And they dedicated themselves to business without going to college.

Some people think that going to college is a great start for a young entrepreneur. But little do they know that you can be $150,000 richer by NOT going to college. You can learn business skills without taking a HUGE loan from the bank and still have enough money to pay your rent!

* * *

See what I did there? This is the type of story that breaks false beliefs. And this is EXACTLY what I want you to do.

Break people false beliefs, break people false beliefs – that's all you have to do!

Remember I said, sell them on the WHY and deliver the HOW. So your Facebook lives should break false beliefs and the course videos should be all about the HOW.

There's a great book by Russell Brunson called *Expert Secrets* where he talks about "breaking false beliefs".

You can get this book at www.geneadam.com/expert

I want you to get that book, and in the book, Russell talks more about how to break false beliefs and the science behind it.

When you try to sell someone on a new opportunity, almost instantly their subconscious mind will start thinking about all the reasons why it isn't possible, or how this wouldn't work for them!

Imagine this: your customer has an experience, and something bad happens to them and then they tell themselves a story that THIS doesn't work. Then, their brain saves that story and it becomes a belief. Over the years we have thousands of these beliefs accumulated in our brains... Some of those beliefs are good, some are not.

For example, let's say your childhood's dream was to be a musician. And then one day your sibling or a friend started laughing at you when you started singing and playing piano. They told you that your "voice sucks" and "can you just shut the hell up and stop playing the piano?" and then unconsciously you told yourself a story you are a "bad" musician, based on someone's opinion. What if they were in a bad mood? Or maybe they joked? Or maybe they are not a musician themselves and they have no musical talent to recognize you "sucked"... So you told yourself a phony story that you suck at singing and that playing piano is hard. So you give up on your dream. See where I am going with this?

The bottom line is, you need to create an "Epiphany Story" or a new story in their head and destroy the old belief. Just simply create a "good" story that replaces the "bad" story in their head. How do you do that? Here's what you can do: "I thought playing piano is hard too until a professional piano player showed me a few chord tricks that you can master within hours, and now everyone is so impressed with my piano skills".

STEPS TO CREATING AN EPIPHANY STORY

Here are the steps how you can create an Epiphany Story:

Step 1. What is the "false" belief your client got?
Step 2. Figure out what experience they have had?
Step 3. What "false" story are they telling themselves?
Step 4. Find a new better story. (It's your job to do the research.)

> If you want to read more about this, go to page 128 in the *Expert Secrets* book. You can get the *Expert Secrets* book here. (source: www.geneadam.com/expert)

So now we know that we need to break "false" beliefs, and we need to structure our content that tells epiphany stories. Those stories will convert lookie-loos into interested buyers…

HUMANIZE YOUR BRAND

Next, you need to humanize your brand and be vulnerable and authentic.

When I say humanize your brand, I mean that people like and follow real people. Real struggles, real life story, real things you deal with in your life. If you tell stories of your failures and what you've learned from them, you can have a lot of "aha" stories to tell... But don't be tempted to talk about your personal problems, how you broke up with your ex and how you got the trauma from it, and some other unrelated drama... This is a BIG no-no. Let me make an example of a Facebook post that would be okay:

* * *

It's dark. My wife just walked in the house. Silence. "You lied to me", the first thing she said. I knew she caught me... "I'm screwed", I thought to myself... Silence. "I trusted you", she cried... "How could you do this to us? Look what I found in the mailbox, these letters!"...

"You spent all of our savings to buy some stupid online courses and you didn't pay off the credit cards... Now we are going to lose our house!"... "My gosh! How could you do this to us?".. My heart sank.. I thought she wouldn't find out.. at least, not so fast.. ...

3 years later me and my wife were sitting on the beach in Maui, Hawaii and I turned to her and said, "Honey, look over there, I just bought that yacht, I called it your name, Mary!"...

* * *

But, it wouldn't be ok to post this:

* * *

He called me a f-!@# b-!@#, he always comes home late, so I know something is wrong, maybe he's got a girlfriend on the side, I think I got it figured out... I spied on him on his phone and he seems to have these weird messages from this girl... Bla bla bla...

* * *

See, vulnerable doesn't mean write anything or make a video live just about anything... It has to mean business. Deep inside there has to be a lesson, something a person reading can improve on.

It can't be some complaining about tra-la-la... No one cares. It has to be educating, giving knowledge to others, and the most important value... It has to be beneficial to the other person...

So, to summarize be authentic, vulnerable, real, but not too much, leave the part of your crazy, personal and inappropriate life out of the public eye unless you can turn that content into a business lesson that your audience can benefit from.

INFLUENCER POSITIONING

Finally, you have to position yourself as an influencer on Facebook. How? Optimize your Facebook Profile. To do that you have to have everything screaming "I'm an influencer in my market"... You profile photo, your profile background image, your bio, the places you work at, Your WHOLE Facebook profile page should look like you are a REAL influencer. Also, your posts, your videos and your photos must match that.

Point the link in your bio and profile image to your Facebook group. In the links section put the link to your FB group as well (even if your group is small).

Perception is reality. If you look like a rip off, everyone will take you as a rip off. If you look like you are a real deal, probably you are a real deal. Don't fake it. But don't show your stupid, or crazy side, or something that is not related to your business. Show your best! People trust successful people whether you like it or not.

Having high numbers also help your positioning. The numbers don't lie. When you have 4,000 followers on your Facebook profile, people tend to trust you more. When you have 1000 subscribers on your YouTube channel that means you have some content that caused people to hit subscribe. If you have 200 likes on a Facebook post that means you said something important there. When you create your content, keep that in mind. When you host a Facebook Live ask them to like, comment, share and follow you.

SUMMARY

To establish YOU as your personal brand, mark the checkboxes you have already completed:

- ☐ Find <u>courage</u> to go on even when you get 0 followers, 0 sales and 0 engagement.
- ☐ Be okay with working for free
- ☐ Overcome your worst fears about being an influencer with your <u>big why</u>. What drives you to be the best version of you?
- ☐ Learn to give away amazing <u>free value</u> via Facebook lives daily
- ☐ Learn to <u>break false beliefs</u> through your content
- ☐ Tell <u>epiphany stories</u> in your posts, FB lives and video

- ☐ Talk about the real life things. Be <u>authentic</u> and <u>vulnerable</u>, but avoid drama
- ☐ Position yourself as an <u>authority</u> in your market space
- ☐ Optimize your Facebook profile
- ☐ Improve the number of likes, comments and followers by asking them for a call to action.

Secret #5
THEM: How to Find Your Perfect Audience

FIND YOUR CUSTOMER AVATAR

Why do we need to find your perfect audience? Because if you don't put out the right message solving the real problem they have, you'll have a hard time selling them on anything.

Ok, so to find your perfect audience means that you need to find your perfect customer avatar. Please don't skip this part even if you think you know what customer avatar is. 95% of people get this part wrong! Plus, I'll go deeper than most gurus do.

Most of the time, the reason you are not making sales is not because you have a bad course, a bad video, or bad content...

but because you don't have the right eyeballs. And if the right people don't see your offer, then you don't have any sales.

Way back when I started I created a course that got 0 sales! Oops… It totally flopped.

Here's why. Instead of creating a course, coaching or training, you first need to find out who your PERFECT CUSTOMER is… I call it the "customer avatar" (or C.A.)

So, to get to your perfect C.A. we have to go 4 levels deep by asking some questions:

LEVEL 1 (novice level) :
- What's their relationship status?
- What's their income?
- Do they have kids?
- How old are they?
- Where do they live?
- Male / Female?

This is too basic and sometimes not as important. So, let's go deeper. Some "gurus" stop here, they think that's all it is. LOL. 😊 But the better gurus don't stop there.

LEVEL 2 (intermediate level) :
- What do they do?
- Where do they work?
- What are they like?
- Do they hate their job?

- Do they hate their boss?
- What are their pains and frustrations?
- What is their big WHY?
- What are their fears?
- What outcome do they desire?
- What needs to change for them so they can start doing what they love?

Some stop here. But I would keep on going. Let's go even deeper.

LEVEL 3 (advanced level) :

Let's walk through his/her day.
- When they open their eyes while they are in bed what do they think first?
- What do they do first? (Be specific. For example, do they hate waking up to the alarm clock?)
- What are they thinking while driving in traffic to work?
- What does their boss think of them?
- They are eating lunch, what do you they think while eating?
- When they come home, what does their family think of them?
- How do they spend their time after work?
- What do they read? Watch TV? What kind of videos do they watch YouTube? What channels?
- When they talk to their spouse what do they talk about?
- What are the personal and family struggles?

- When they have a headache what is it about?

Dig deeper, almost there.

LEVEL 4 (superior level) :
- What is the ONE THING your product can do for THEM that will change THEIR life based on the Level 1,2,3?
- What is the urgent need that will be filled after they purchase your program based on the Level 1,2,3?
- Is the need URGENT? If not, find the urgent need… It will be 10x easier to sell… Example, "my head hurts, please give me a medicine for that right away…"
- How will their life improve after they use your product based on the level 1,2,3? Show undeniable results of other people you have already helped.

Bonus questions to help you find out your C.A.:

How are your competitors selling to them? (spy on the competitors)
- What 'special' language does your customer use to describe the existing problem or frustration? It could be a different language than you speak in your niche.

To download the PDF and print it out with all of the customer avatar levels and questions, go to www.geneadam.com/avatar

WHERE IS MY AUDIENCE?

So the theory is nice and all, but where can you find your audience?

When I first started I thought that the internet traffic was like a water facet. You open the facet and the traffic comes out just like water… LOL 😂😂😂 No really. I thought that. I know that was dumb.

Then one day, I told my mentor about what I thought the internet traffic was and he burst into laughter. And then he told me a story. It went like this.

Just imagine the ocean. There is fish. Different colors: red, yellow and blue ones. While there's plenty of fish, you have to attract the right fish. So, the red fish is hanging out in places where there is lot of other red fish.

And so, people are the same. People that like cooking are probably hanging out in the same FB Group about cooking. People that love marketing are probably in their own FB group about marketing. People that like racing cars are congregated in another Facebook group. There are many different spots they are hanging out at and so you can always find places where to find them.

In some Facebook groups there are hundreds of thousands of your potential customers at once! And so, you want to be in front of them. And you know what? You got to give them what they want.

You got to write specifically designed long posts that make people like, comment and engage with you. I'll call these posts the "bait" so I can illustrate my point. I'll talk how to construct these posts later.

So, you have to throw the "bait" in the group where your perfect customers are, sit back, relax, and watch the hungry fish attack your bait with likes and comments… Get some popcorn, and start commenting on your posts. Then, people will come to your profile and check you out and if you are the person they need, then you got yourself a potential customer. Are you getting this?

And here's where almost everyone gets it wrong (95% of you). Most throw the bait all over the place… and hope it works but… it doesn't. You get zero engagement, zero followers and zero sales. The problem is that most don't throw the bait in the right places.

Here's an example. There's a group on Facebook called *Advertise Anything*, so you advertise there and no one clicks on your link. Why? Wrong place. Then you drop your link in 100 other places and no one buys there either. Hmm… 😂😂😂 Then you say, "It just doesn't work! I'm quitting!" 😰

It's not the quantity. It's not the gazillion of unrelated people. You just need 100 very targeted people and you won't need to sell them hard even if the price of your course is $697… Let me do the math just so you know it ain't peanuts $697*100=$69,700

We need to put the bait in the right places and get as many eyeballs as possible. To get the right people that would like what you offer, pick a few targeted Facebook groups in your niche, join those groups and voila you are a part of the network.

When you create a bait for your potential customers keep in mind about the things that can go wrong:
1. Wrong headline/ad
2. Wrong audience
3. Wrong story
4. Wrong offer or no offer at all (most of the time the offer comes later, not with the bait)

Always check these.

Headlines should be sharp to the point. Audience should already expect somebody to come around and save them. Your offer should be so bright and irresistible, they just don't have a choice but pull out the credit card and buy from you. I'll cover more on this in the coming chapters.

To summarize, we have found "THEM", your audience. Here's the list of things that we have completed:

- ☐ Created your Customer Avatar (C.A.) We Went 4 levels deep. If you don't have a perfect customer avatar in your head you almost NEVER will sell anything to anyone. Don't be broad. "Selling to everyone - will sell to no one".
- ☐ We found where on the internet your perfect audience is hiding.

- [ ] We learned how you can create a "bait" that you will use to engage with people and drive them to your personal page.
- [ ] Look for groups that are in your niche and join them, and post you're your stories and educational content there.

Secret #6
Find and Validate Their PROBLEM

For some reason this one has been one of the most overlooked and underrated mistakes almost every entrepreneur makes. Why they just don't learn? 😊

What are you going to do if your idea flops?

People create products without validating their idea and without asking their market whether they need it or would pay for it.

90% of people say THEY KNOW WHAT their customer needs. They say, "I don't need to validate my idea. I got 20 years of experience and from what I know THIS will work". Really? And you won't validate if anyone will actually pull out the credit card and pay for your product?

Do you want me to tell you the truth? It's proven that most of us suck at predicting. And because we think we know, we don't validate. If you want to find out why we suck at it, read a great book called *The Black Swan* by Nassim Taleb. Our guesses are as good as flipping a coin with a 50/50 chance.

There are 2 things you need to validate:
- If there's a problem that needs to be solved
- If people would actually pay for it (in some cases they won't pay)

QUICK VALIDATION FORMULA

1. Ask people, what is your biggest problem in [*the niche*]. They say, X.
2. Drill down. Ask them the second question: "What is your biggest struggle when it comes to X? They say Y.
3. Tell them you are going to deliver Y in a few days and give them the link.
4. Set up an order page that says if you pay $___ for the beta product you will get Y and save 50%. The only caveat of the beta is that you will get it next week. But in exchange you can save 50% if you order today.
5. After people paid for it and you received the money in your hand, go and create the product that solves Y.

I've seen this formula working thousands of times on FB Personal Profiles and Facebook Groups.

So let's go through this formula in detail.

VALIDATION FORMULA - STEP 1

To get this step done we must find their problem. You need to ask them the question: "What is the biggest problem you have right now?", but if they don't answer you have to be smarter.

You don't have to ask them straight, but you can write a post to see if people are interested in that. Post them on your Personal Profile or your Facebook Group.

This is how it would look in a Facebook post:

* * *

"Hey! I'm working on a perfect Facebook Live template that'll help you crush with Facebook Lives...who wants in? Comment "Gimme, the template" below!"
- OR -
"Hey! If I showed you the exact step by step system I used to launch & sell my course to 30+ people in the first 15 days would you be interested? "
- OR -
"Who in here has a Facebook group and wants to monetize it? Comment 🖐"

* * *

These examples got good results. But it really depends on your audience. Don't just copy them, change them. The goal is not to repeat but learn how to do it yourself so you can do it for years to come. I promise you, the more you do it the easier it gets.

VALIDATION FORMULA - STEP 2

So now you should see the response. Some of these posts won't have interest at all. Move on to the next topic if no one liked it or commented on it. Every audience is different so it doesn't mean that the topic is bad. It's just not relatable to your audience.

Let's say one of our posts got likes and comments. Let's say it's about Facebook lives. We can make a new post and say:

* * *

"Hey guys, what are you struggling with most when it comes to Facebook Lives?

* * *

They will comment and say, "I'm not comfortable on camera.", "I hate looking at myself on the video". "I can't do it because I suck on camera." Those are the problems people really have.

VALIDATION FORMULA - STEP 3

It looks like you got some answers. Now we are going to tell them that we are creating the course and if they want to get it, they will get 50% off.

* * *

"Hey guys! I'm going to film a Facebook Live course this weekend about how to be confident and not suck on Facebook Lives ...who wants it?
Comment "FB Rocks" below and I'll hook you up!"

* * *

VALIDATION FORMULA - STEP 4

Make a page that lets them purchase this course for 50% off. It can be anywhere from $97-$497.

SUMMARY

So, by finding what their PROBLEM is and validating if people will pay for it, we achieved two things:

#1. You don't have to spend too much time to create a course that could potentially flop. If you would spend 6 months creating it, you would not get a penny from it if it fails.

#2. You got the money before creating the course! Who wouldn't like to get paid in advance and then do the work? Yes, you still need to create an awesome course, that's a given. But, It's easier to create a course with cash in your hand than without.

Just this secret is worth $10K, especially if you can implement it right away. Do you remember the Promise Note in the beginning of the book? You promised to implement it and this secret can help you do exactly that! Ok? Please implement it and do it and you will be awesome!

Secret #7
How to Write Your STORY

WHY YOUR STORY IS IMPORTANT?

Ok, so now we are going to create your story. Why writing your story is important? Let me explain. A long time ago when you were a kid, you probably still can remember you mom telling you stories. All kids love stories, don't they? When we grow up we still love stories.

Star Wars? Titanic? Avatar? What do they have to do with selling? Everything. These movies are memorable, they sit in your memory for a lifetime and they are super lucrative.

Star Wars movies combined have earned over $4 billion.
Titanic movie alone has made over $1.8 billion.
Avatar movie has earned over $2.7 billion.

Titanic movie lasted only 3 hours 15 minutes and *Avatar* - 2 hours and 42 minutes. And within those 3 hours our mind transported into a different reality where our emotions and feelings took over and we lived through a virtual life of our favorite characters. We came out of the movie theater happy and gladly parted with our $10. Along the way, we made all the people involved in the movie a lot of cash… Screen writers, designers, actors, directors and so on.

So, what am I saying here? Are people crazy to waste $10 in the movie theater on some made-up story and the next time they are glad to do that again? 😂😂😂 Yep! That's exactly what I am saying.

The stories sell all around us. They are on the news, in the ads, in the history class, and in Facebook Posts and Lives. Most of the time we like them, comment on them, share them and buy what that story sells us. Big brands, religion and even countries tell us a story with a couple of words.

Ferrari's story? Luxury and fast cars.

Mercedes? Class and style.

Bible? Faith in Christianity.

Hawaii? Beach.

Japan? Sushi.

France? Champagne.

Italy? Spaghetti.

It's endless…

All these associations are created by the stories that were told to us a long time ago. The story is the closest thing to the real-life experience we have. If the story is set up correctly it can change people's minds and make people believe in new things. In the Secret #4 we learned how to break your customer's "false" beliefs, and here we will craft a story that will talk to THEM directly.

HOW TO CRAFT YOUR STORY

There's a *StoryBrand* book by Donald Miller and below I will give you the most important formula that you need to know from that book.

Story Brand Formula

1. Character
2. Problem
3. Guide
4. Plan
5. Calls to action
6. Results into something
7. Success or Failure

For example, the "character" has a "problem" with Facebook Lives. They are scared to be on the camera and that becomes a HUGE problem, because deep inside they tell themselves they will never do this and so they "hit the wall".

And what do you think happens next? They usually go on a journey to find an answer how to solve their problem. They look everywhere and nothing seems to work.

They finally find somebody who can show them the ropes. So, our "character" finds this girl who's really good at Facebook Lives. She's an awesome coach ("guide") and she teaches the "character" how to be really good at Facebook Lives.

She teaches the "plan". And now our "character" has to try this and do the Facebook Lives on their own.

So the character has a "calling" and then something really bad happens. The character ran out of money and now they MUST make money with Facebook Lives and start selling products online. In other words, they just have to succeed with the plan that the "guide" gave them.

The "character" tries it and gets on a Facebook live. They try once, twice, three times and suddenly they started making money online. And that turned into a HUGE "success".

* * *

Ok, next let me show you how this formula can work in a movie and then we will come back and try to apply this in your business.

By the way, every successful movie has this type of story structure and every successful business has that too.

First, let me show you how this formula works in a movie, and then how it can work in business and then I will explain it.

In *Star Wars* it worked this way:

1. Character: *Luke Skywalker*
2. Problem: *The Death Star*
3. Guide: *Yoda*
4. Plan: *Yoda taught him to "trust the force"*
5. Call to action: *He has to fight, or it will destroy them.*
6. Result: *They fight*
7. Success? *Yes! They destroy the Death Star*

If you notice in the movie it has all of these elements. These elements keep us engaged and they keep us intrigued. "You always wonder what will happen in the end of the movie? It's so good, I need to finish watching it!"

Ok, now I will make an example in business. In the #2 bullet, I will split it into 3 parts. <u>Internal</u> problem, <u>External</u> problem and <u>Philosophical</u> problem. That's because we usually deal with more than 1 problem in our heads. Sometimes 1 problem to a solution works for them, but sometimes they need a bigger kick in the butt to come through.

<u>Internal</u> problem is what's going on in your head.
<u>External</u> problem means it's the actual physical problem.
And <u>Philosophical</u> is what you believe in and stand for.

In a *Weight Loss Business* it can work like this:
1. Character: *Jane Smith. She wants to be liked and accepted.*

2. Internal Problem: *She hates the feeling that when she is in bikini, she looks ugly on the beach when people look at her.*
   External Problem: *Lose weight*
   Philosophical: *She wants to have a healthy lifestyle and keep up with the children when they grow up.*
3. Guide: *Trainer Scott*
4. Plan: *Step by step 6-week work out plan*
5. Call to action: *Meeting every Monday at 2pm*
6. Result: *Slow but incremental improvements*
7. Success? *Yes! She lost 7 pounds*

And now let me compare the movie and the business example in more detail side by side.

So *The Character* in the movie is the protagonist Luke Skywalker whereas in your business it is <u>THEM: Your Customer</u> and from the Secret #5 you already know who your customer is, right?

Next, *The Problem* is a bit trickier because it's got 3 parts:
- Internal (what's going on in your customer's mind)
- External (what their problem actually is)
- Philosophical (how the problem should work out on a global scale, what your customer believes in and what they stand for)

The movie also has Internal, External and Philosophical problems but to make things super simple I specified just one external problem which is *The Death Star*. So here you need to come up with those 3 problems.

Then, we got *The Guide,* this is almost never the Hero… The Guide is a usually a teacher or a mentor, or somebody that can see in things what the Hero cannot see…

In the movie it's Yoda. In the business example it was trainer Scott. In your business it's probably <u>YOU.</u>

Next, there got to be a *Plan*. Without the plan nothing works. You can give a 5-Step Blueprint to whatever you are selling. Give them a tangible plan they can follow and succeed.

Then, make them take action with *The Call to Action*. "Buy the course by Friday 11:59pm for $297 ~~$997~~" will work, but make it as genuine and believable as possible. Always give them a good reason to take massive action. Many people fail at this and create cheesy offers.

And then, there are *The Results*. This is where you take your testimonials and put them in here. And the more results and testimonials you get, the more sales you get. You need to show your potential clients what kind of results you can get them.

It's worth collecting a lot of *The Success Stories* as well, because potential customers love hearing the case studies of people who walked through the same path before them.

You can use your crafted stories in the long written Facebook posts, Facebook lives, webinars, books, courses and just about anything.

DRAMATIC STORIES

Make your stories as emotional as possible. That's the key. Stale stories suck. Move, emote, create amazing energy. Don't forget – the best stories are:
1. Scary
2. Tragic
3. Dramatic
4. Emotional
5. Vivid
6. Authentic
7. Vulnerable
8. Real

The stories don't have to be true in movies but in your business they should be. If you don't have results yet, then go back to the Secret #4 and read the paragraph WORK FOR FREE.

To sell via Facebook Lives is super easy today. The good news is that you already have this "thing" called phone that has a camera on it. You got the actor/actress – YOU, you got the director, also YOU, and the cameraman / camerawoman – it happens to be YOU as well. And now you just need the STORY. Go and create it.

Secret #8
How to SELL Without Selling

SELL ON EMOTION, NOT LOGIC

Most of you do this backwards and sell on logic! Usually it goes like this:

First, you hear about something from your parents, your friends, TV, YouTube or any other media. And then you get excited. In fact, you get SO excited, the blood starts rushing through your body. Wow, you say, if I could just learn this one thing I can be the happiest person on the planet earth. And then you do. You start learning everything about it.

You learn the skill and become really good at what you do. But then you become so smart at it, you go so deep that your lingo changes and you lose the touch with simplicity. You lose the ability to explain things the easy way. *(I'll cover how to talk simpler like a 6 year-old in just a little bit.)*

You start spewing the jargon left and right and no one, I mean, NO ONE cares about what you say, because they don't get it.

And then you lose them. You don't make any sales. You wonder why can't they see this? If they only can see this. This product is SO good for them!

You can show them numbers, graphs, pictures. You can tell them that they will make millions of dollars, lose weight, eat great food, etc. But.. most of the time it doesn't work.

Here's probably the most important skill you need to master if you want to make 6 figures and above:

> If you want people to buy your new idea, DON'T give them the answer. Lead them to the answer with your STORY and let them come up with that idea by themselves.

Your story has to lead them to the AHA moment. To the realization. To something where they can learn something.

And then they will come up with the idea to buy your product by themselves.

I call it the "AHA Story"!

It's almost like there are two stories happening in your customer's head instead of just one, emotional and logical.

Let me draw you a picture. You have two stories next to each other. One line is the "emotional" story and the second line is the "logical" story.

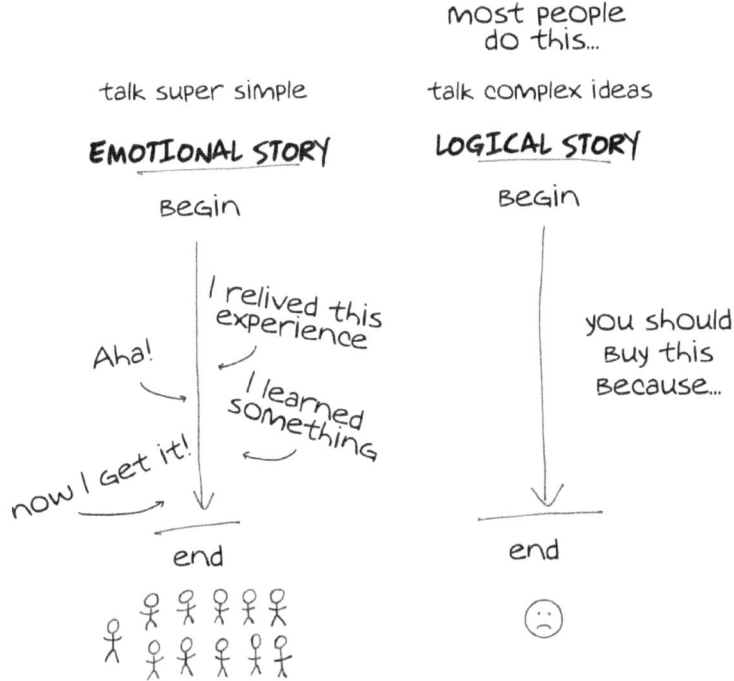

What happens is that they get to the AHA moment in the emotional story and in logical they don't!

For example, do you remember when you got started? What excited you the most about what you do? Tell that "AHA story". Tell them how you felt, what emotions you had at that very moment. Make them dramatic but true!

If you are not sure how to craft a good emotional story you can go back to the previous secret about stories and go through the script one more time. Pay attention to the "Internal problem", because that's the one that makes it emotional.

Don't forget to use very simple language in your stories because people lose you right away. Make it so simple that a 6-year old can understand.

EDUSELLING

Another great way to sell is to educate people.

I want to introduce you to EDU-SELLING. Educating + Selling.

Has it ever happened to you when somebody told you a story about a product and you started wanting it so badly, that you went to the store and bought it?

So, imagine, you are sitting in a café and you have a conversation with your good friend that you trust. She tells you a story about this new restaurant in town with such delicious pizza and let's say you are a pizza lover.. So your friend says: "But, this is not just another pizza it's high level stuff… The cook is from France, cheese is from Switzerland and the truffle… The most incredible type of truffle in the world is the Alba white truffle. When you think of expensive truffles that are very valuable and hard to find. They're incredibly rare, and their flavor is like nothing else in the world of cooking ingredients. And that's what makes Alba white truffle so amazing… I've never tasted anything like that.."

And right after this story, you start thinking about trying this place. And if you don't mind paying for some good food that's the place you are going to go next if you feel like a good tasting pizza.

So, in some of your Facebook Lives, videos and stories you can do the same. All you have to do is two things: Educate + Sell.

However, don't make these mistakes when you edu-sell, because I see them a lot:

1. You only educate, but you don't sell. The ratio should be around 90% education /10% selling
2. You use complicated language
3. Your material is boring

I see a lot of people educating non-stop but they don't have an offer ready. Your offer has to be ready before you start educating. I made this mistake and it bit me in the ass… Always be selling. Saying that, you still can educate and you don't have to sell them anything while you're growing a HUGE following, but why wouldn't you have something ready so you can make money too?

Next, educate people without any complicated language. As soon as you use technical words you lose them. It needs to flow with ease as you are talking to a 6-year old child.

TALK TO THEM LIKE A 6 YEAR-OLD

One time I mentored somebody who was using complicated language A LOT. Let's call him Malcolm, for privacy reasons. And Malcolm's goal was to explain what 'funnel' meant. He kept on telling me abstract words and I couldn't bear it anymore. I kept on asking him to dumb it down and still no luck.

"Do you have children?", I asked.

"Yes, I do. I have a 6-year-old daughter."

"Good. So why don't you talk to your daughter tonight and explain to her what 'funnel' means and call me in the morning".

"What? She won't understand me", he said.

"Well just try it, what do you have to lose? Describe it to her in the language she understands, simplify the words for her, and then just write it all down".

He didn't believe me at first, but then he said, "Ok" and hung up.

Next morning he said, "Wow, my daughter now knows what I do. I could never tell her what I do".

"Really?", I said.

"Yes! She understands 'funnels' now."

"That's exciting", I said, "So what did you tell her?"

"I asked her if she knew what a web page is and when she said yes, I said a 'funnel' is just many connected webpages that lead to a buy button and when people click that button, we ship them our product".

Then I asked him, "could she explain it in her own words after you explained it?"

"Yep! She told me what 'funnel' is in her own words! And then she said that she wants a funnel too!"

* * *

Have a casual conversation. Tell your story in the simplest words that even a 6-year old could understand... That includes your written story, Facebook lives, videos, posts, ads or any content you produce. That way you won't lose customers left and right just because of a language disconnect.

YOU ARE IN THE BUSINESS OF SERVING, NOT SELLING

Great businesses focus on serving, not selling. It's like in a restaurant. Who likes to be served poorly? Anybody?

You are waiting in the restaurant to be seated for a dinner with your date for half an hour! Finally, an angry girl comes up, doesn't smile and mumbles, "come with me". You order your food dealing with her bad attitude like you are bothering her or something. And then... the worst happened. She brings the plate and literally almost throws it in your face... The plate slid on the table and almost hit you! You angrily ask her, "What just happened? Why are you so upset?". She says "Nothing. I'm just doing my job!". (True story by the way!)

This is exactly what 80% of people are doing in any type of business, they are "just doing their job." Because they don't care, but they really should care! Customers will never come back for businesses that don't serve. Treat them as royalty, as your family and they will come back again and again.

If you want to be an influencer that people care about, then don't "just do your work", but serve them well.

So, how can you serve them well? Give them free complimentary items. Give them free bonuses (if you buy X, I will give you Y). Give them free consultations. And give them the best impression of you.

In fact, serving them works so well, it can 10X your conversions. You know why it works so well? Because almost nobody does it… Just remember this: "To sell is to serve."

ALWAYS HAVE YOUR OFFER READY

Have an irresistible offer ready to go, because you never know when your next customer wants to get what you sell.

For all I know, your customer Jane could be having thoughts about buying what you sell, but if you don't offer her anything, she is gone! And she will buy it from someone else.

Maybe Jane wants to learn how to play a guitar, or maybe she wants a haircut, or maybe Jane wants to buy a workout plan from you, or maybe she wants some business coaching, or maybe she wants a new funnel, or maybe she wants to hire you as a Facebook agency to help her sell condos that are worth $100,000 each?

But if you don't offer anything and leave this task for later then even if you have 1 gazillion people it doesn't count until you make a sale.

When your cart is open and you are open for business you can start having money coming in. If you don't have this part ready, it doesn't matter how much content you create it's all useless.

Many of my students create amazing content, but they don't have anything to sell yet. That means that if you do have a lot of free content already, you need to be ready to offer something that people can buy. Otherwise you won't make money. Period. As a rule of thumb, you should have 90% free content and 10% pitching. You can simply introduce a paid offer by mentioning it in the end of your FB lives.

ALWAYS BE SELLING

I don't mean to say every 5 minutes "buy my stuff", "buy my stuff" like a parrot. NO! That's not how to do this right. And I don't mean to spam your links on your wall, in other Facebook groups and Facebook Messenger. That's not how you sell.

What I mean by always be selling is to structure your free content the way that effortlessly sells your paid stuff. Sometimes you don't even have to sell it hard. If your offer is sexy it can sell on its own by mentioning it once or twice.

Here are some great offers from a few influencers.

Peng Joon wrote this Facebook ad that got a lot of attention and a link on the bottom to his offer:

* * *

1) Wake up inspired 1) Wa 🦉

2) Watch videos from Grant, Gary and the other G's 📱

3) The G's ain't rolling in 💰

4) You remind yourself it's all about the hustlin and the grindin 🔥

5) There's no clients so you offer free "strategy sessions" to potential clients hoping to close them 📞

6) You are now fully booked 🗓

7) Your calendar looks like a jail cell with all those bars 🔒

8) You hate your boss but you realise that you are the boss 🙈

9) First client of the day is a no show 👻

10) You try to squeeze in a quick meal before the next client 🍔

11) You're on the call but you realize you have to pee 🙈

12) You pee on the sides of the bowl hoping to mask the sound 😶

13) After 30 minutes your potential client says "I'll think about it" 😡

14) You finally get a query from Sukhdeep in India 🇮🇳

15) Instead, Sukhdeep sells you a website 🖥

16) You now have a website that looks beautiful but does absolutely nothing 🕸

17) You write a couple of blog posts ✏️

18) You post on Facebook 👍

19) You get 2 likes (your mum and dad) 👨‍👩

20) You keep going 🏃

21) You remind yourself that it's about the hustle and grind 🧟

22) You take a picture of yourself on a laptop hustling and grinding 🔥

23) You add in hashtags #entrepreneur #hustling #grinding #nevergiveup 🏃

24) You realize nobody cares 🤷

25) You ask yourself if you even care 🤔

26) Facebook and Instagram change their algorithm 😤

27) Nobody sees your posts anymore 😒

28) Not even Sukhdeep from India 👳

Or... you can get this FREE book instead and discover how to close on sales videos, webinars or live events, without all of the headaches above.

Click here to claim your FREE copy ==> http://www.hissite.com

* * *

And here's another post that I liked. This Facebook post got a bunch of action with "comment below" call-to-action in the end:

* * *

🔥Free Training Tomorrow🔥:

"How I built a $65,000 a Month Facebook group, And how you can do the same (Or better)"

Hey guys, Tomorrow as a for 4th of July Special 🇺🇸, I will be running a JAM PACKED training on the hottest biggest opportunity right now to become wealthy from online marketing.

Transparency time:

❗ There's a reason Why Agency owners are now opening Facebook groups (Hint: they make 10x more with a group than their agency).

Look, You can struggle trying to make agency stuff work and making a bunch of local business owners rich (while they take a shit on you and your work)

Or you can make a bunch of money (20-50k+/M) And have people loving you and appreciating you. ❗

If you miss on this opportunity you really really hate money.

What Will we cover:

✅ How to find a profitable nitch

✅ How to get 1000 people within the next month or two to your group for FREE (Those are highly targeted people, not fillers)

✅ How to trick Facebook algorithms to grow your groups for you

❗ The C.E.M Method ❗

✅ The profile Funnel

✅ The hidden waitlist (Less the %1) people know about this

✅ The reverse Social Selling method I used to hit 60k+ months again and again

✅ The case study on how I took 21 people to 6 figures using those exact method

This is a Limited Number Event.

If you want to save a spot:

1) Comment "60k Months"

2) like this post

I will pm you with a private invite. Let's Go!

* * *

"ONION OFFERS": DON'T SELL PRODUCTS, SELL IRRESISTIBLE OFFERS

What's the difference?

Product is just a bare item. Offer is a bundle. Add something to your product and make it an offer.

You don't buy just a car for cash. Almost no one does. You buy a car, finance it, get insurance, and they upsell you on the limited edition.

You don't buy a burger you get fries and a drink with it.

So how do you create an irresistible offer?

Irresistible. What a tricky word. Food could be irresistible. For women, Italian cannoli with pieces of chocolate on top can look so delicious, that they can't stop looking, they just got to eat it. (women almost always can relate to that one). For guys it could be a beautiful suit, or a sexy car? Most guys would die for having status and money in the bank.

Irresistible offer. It's something that your customer can't say no to. What is it in your market space that would make it irresistible? It's an offer you can't refuse, just like in the movie *The God Father*, but without a bullet to your head... With pure psychology and on your customer's terms!

What is it so delicious, amazing, ridiculously awesome that no one else offers? It almost feels like you (the seller) lose more than the buyer.

It's walking on the fine line that can make you extreme amounts of money, because everybody wants it and they can't get it anywhere...

One of the easiest ways to do that is to shower your customers with a bunch of bonuses... Bonuses are like freebies that come with it, but they cost a lot! Include those juicy value bonuses that are worth $100, $1000, or even $10000!

Here's a rule of thumb you can use when you create an offer:

Always Sell "ONION" Offers

To help you with irresistible offers think of an onion. The onion is ONE OFFER. But then you start peeling the onion and you get a bunch of layers.

In the middle is your product. And the layers are your bonuses and the whole thing is an offer. Sell that!

Give them 3-5 bonuses... Give them the cheat sheet, the e-book and the interview you did the other day... And tell them it's going to be available for a few hours / days only...

Sometimes it's worth making bonuses as good as the actual product!

Here are a few simple examples of extra bonuses:

- A 14-day trial to a $300 software? That's a huge value of ($150 value)
- 15-minute free coaching call? ($200 value)
- A free funnel you can create for somebody and get paid on the backend. ($1000 value)

But make sure you show it to the right people. Here's the magic formula:

> The Right Audience + Incredibly Amazing Value That They Would Be Stupid Not To Take = Offer You Can't Refuse

To skyrocket your sales you might have to do something even better. You might give them a promise that is almost TOO GOOD TO BE TRUE. Work on it. Think what else you can give them. Take time, think about it and you might strike gold.

Look at what the Domino's Pizza did. Here's one of the best too-good-to-be-true offers I have ever heard:

"Domino's Pizza offers a pizza in 30 minutes or less… or it's free."

They are willing to give you money back 100% if they are late! Wow, that's what I call walking on the line of losing everything to the customer, if they don't deliver… And that's irresistible!

Here's a Facebook Post that I just saw on my timeline from a very good internet marketer that I like. Every time he does it, I get excited:

* * *

"Comment The Advice You Would
Give Yourself 5 Years Ago
Best Advice Gets $997 Course"

* * *

BONUSES

Create a lot of bonuses for people (3 to 5 bonuses) no matter what you sell. Just shower people with bonuses.

Find anything that they might need and give it to them. It could be:

- Video trainings, Web classes, Mini courses
- Templates
- Cheatsheets, Worksheets or Checklists
- E-books or PDFs

- Physical Books or Brochures
- Audio Interviews (or video)
- Photoshop Design Files
- Ipads or any electronic item (if the budget allows)
- T-shirts, Flashlights
- Cars (yes, some big influencers give away cars)

Also you can create anything that can save them time and money. Your bonuses must stand out. Make it such a no brainer for people that they don't have a choice but buy your stuff.

Make sure that you create bonuses that your customers most struggle with. **When you go back to the secret #6 about their problems you'll discover so many possible solutions you can create for your customers. It's a goldmine.**

As my mentor says create bonuses as good as, or better than the products you sell. Make them so desirable that they can't say no.

CONFIDENCE

Confidence is one of those things that makes people believe that you know enough about the product you're selling.

When people are about to buy from you, they want to make sure they are not making a mistake. And confidence does it almost every time. It puts you up as an authority in your customer's eyes.

When you think of a doctor, does he talk confidently? When you think of a teacher and she tells you what to do confidently, do you obey?

If she was not a confident teacher, she was probably not a good teacher in the first place. Students will scream over teachers like that and they can never teach well.

We respect authority and authority talks to us the way that we respect them and we think that they're knowledgeable because they're so confident. They look like they know, so we think that they know too. Why? Because perception is reality.

Confidence is something you should inject in your marketing for sure. You don't have to manipulate people. That's not what I'm talking about here. What I'm saying is that if you believe that your product is helpful for your customers then there's no reason why you shouldn't be confident.

Here's the thing. If you are not confident, people start thinking stories in their head, like, "why is this person not confident about their product?", "is the product not good enough?", "is there something wrong?" So, if you're not confident, people just won't buy from you.

Even if you have some confidence it still can work out alright, but if you don't have any confidence, that's when you will look bad and you will make zero sales.

On the flip side, when you're too confident you don't have to be cocky and bossy. You should come out as a knowledgeable person like a doctor.

Here's an example of how to screw up as a marketer when you try to sell something. Imagine this scenario.

You are waiting for your doctor in the hospital. The doctor comes in and tells you, "er…, we have to cut your stomach."

"Why, doctor?", you ask.

"I think it's your liver, it could be your heart but I think it's your liver… Let's do the surgery on your liver first and then if it doesn't fix it, then we should do the surgery on the heart. Frankly, I'm not sure which one should be first, but it probably doesn't matter anyway". Would you trust this guy ???

So, become an authority like a real doctor. Just be confident and it does the trick.

SOCIAL PROOF

Social proof sounds kind of complicated when you hear it first…proof? what? But it's really not that hard.

Social proof is when people talk good about you and you build the name for yourself by doing that. To make people talk about you, all you have to do is to show them great results.

If you were Steve Jobs and people already know that you create awesome computers, it's easier to sell them on more computers, right? If you were Billy Holiday can you sell us on some more awesome jazz? What would be the probability of Michael Jackson coming out with a new hit song?

If you have a lot of great results and testimonials and people rave about you it will be an easy sell. But how do you show them your results if you don't have any? You need to get them. Work for free and ask your client if you can share the results.

Otherwise it's a catch 22 and you will never get out of misery just because you don't have the results to show so you can't sell, but to sell you need the results.

There are 4 steps to get social proof.

1. Find a person/company for whom you can work for free
2. Get results in exchange for testimonials.
3. Collect testimonials, results and case studies.
4. Show your results to your potential customers.

So, make it a goal to collect your testimonials in a folder and when the time is right pull them out from your folder and show them to your customers.

When you sell a product on your sales page, show screenshots of your results and video testimonials right next to your buy buttons.

Doing interviews can help you boost your social proof as well. If you associate your name with other big names in the industry, people will start thinking highly of you and buy more of your stuff.

Also, you can get social proof by showing up in the media, like Huffington Post, Entrepreneur, and even Forbes magazine. Find connections and show up anywhere you can and it will help you to grow your brand exponentially.

SCARCITY

Scarcity is a great tool, but you must use it right. You can either 10x your sales with it or lose all of your customers. Weird right? It sure is.

If people spot it's a fake, they will run as quickly as possible because they will think you are trying to trick them.

"Only 7 spots left", you say... Really? How come your page still says 7 spots left and you already announced you have made 20 sales? Hm... 😊😊😊 Either I don't know how to count or I smell something fishy.

Having legitimate scarcity will solve this problem. You can have product scarcity or time scarcity.

Here is an example of scarcity that could increase your sales:

"I printed only 7 copies of my awesome book and they are waiting to be shipped out of my living room. Because I have only 7 copies left, you should get a copy now, because the next batch of these books will be available in 4 weeks from now, bla, bla, bla. "

And here's another one:

"Today is my birthday and I'm doing something very special. I'm going to sell my course for only $197 (normally $497) and it's going to be available only until 12:00 midnight. Tomorrow It will be back to $497. You have 9 hours left."

SECTION THREE:
CREATING CONTENT

In this section, I will cover how to do FB Lives and write effective posts.

When you write posts and do FB lives don't forget to tell stories as I talked about in the Secret #7. You'll be more fun. If you teach without stories, some people will get bored and leave. Don't be that guy/girl! ☺

One of the most important elements when you create any type of content is to break people's beliefs.

Your content should always:
- Tell Stories
- Break False Beliefs
- Have Massive Value (90% free value and 10% pitching)

Break your customer's "false beliefs", while delivering value. You can teach some secrets but always introduce some elements of false beliefs they might have and break them.

Find something they "believe in" that you know is far away from the truth and teach them why it isn't so.

In other words, find a phony story they are telling themselves and teach them the new story that can achieve amazing results on steroids.

Why do you need to do that? Because people find reasons why [whatever you sell] wouldn't work. That's why people don't buy from you right away and some would never buy from you at all.

Secret #9
What Kind of Content Should You Create?

Just to give you a few ideas what type of content you can create.

You content should:
- teach
- motivate
- build your brand
- build authority
- handle their objections
- solve their problems
- entertain (tie it to what you sell)
- controversy (stay away from politics)

- be polarizing (don't be afraid to stand up what you believe it, people respect people that are real and stand up for themselves)
- show your personality, who you really are
- make them laugh, make them cry
- make them feel something
- show them how you live
- talk about personal adventure / family / team
- show them how you work
- engage (about the topics in your niche)
- show them the process, how you do what you do, your skill
- show them how you are getting from point A to point B in your business and personal life
- give out awesome and value packed free items like PDFs, videos, web trainings, mini-courses, cheat sheets, check lists and other docs that later leads them to your paid stuff
- show them testimonials of other people that succeeded and ask for the new testimonials too
- show them case studies
- show them your results, screen shots
- show social proof of your team's success
- invite them to try your product, subscription or course
- invite them to a beta course
- invite them to a launch of your low ticket offer (and sometimes high ticket offer too)

- invite them to a waiting list before you launch your product
- let them win your course or something they desire by commenting to your post or your FB live
- invite them to get on a 15 minute coffee date (skype about problems they might have in their business. These are usually free)
- discuss something about them
- sell

Important: Tie all of these to what you sell.

Secret #10
How to Come Up with Wanted Content for Facebook Lives

If you truly understand everything we have talked about in the book, I promise this part will be easy.

Start with the content that is relatable in your market. Teach them and break their beliefs. I want to talk about hook, story and transformation.

HOOK, STORY, TRANSFORMATION

There's a formula that I use all the time called *Hook, Story, Transformation*.

Hook is the headline. It's how you interest the people and get them to your Facebook Live.

And the *Story* has to be interesting enough, so it creates a *Transformation* in your listener's mind. Just tell stories that break false beliefs.

How? It's easy.

What I want you to do is to create a *Hook,* one interesting piece, that you can talk about, and then tell a *Story* about it. Tell a story that someone can learn from and that will create a transformation and break their false beliefs.

For example, do you remember my story about how I lost my business and how I didn't build my personal brand and what I learned from it?

This is exactly what I am talking about. I told you how I had a successful business making $26K/month and then my jealous supplier stopped selling me the product. So, what I learned was **I didn't build my personal brand, and this was my biggest mistake.** That was the epiphany. That was the AHA story! That made you realize that you need to build your personal brand and become an influencer, see?

Use this formula: *Hook, Story, Transformation* and tell stories as much as you can on your Facebook Lives.

All of the content you put out has to be wanted and valuable in your niche. So, start with the content that's relatable in your market. Teach them and break their beliefs.

All Facebook lives have to generate as much engagement as possible. The more likes, comments and shares you have the more people on Facebook will see you.

HOW TO BE CONFIDENT ON FACEBOOK LIVES

It's really all about practice. The more you do it the more confident you become, the more comfortable you become with shooting videos...

Everyone can do it but all you have to do is start and continue doing that for the next 90 days or even for 1 year for the best results.

It's like playing a piano. First you suck and then you suck less and then, you actually become really good.

It's like writing in English. First you scribbled and no one could read it, not even you. 😊 And then, you actually got pretty good at it.

Put all your fears aside, have "your WHY bigger than your fears" as we talked about in the Secret #4.

Turn on your phone, laptop, desktop, tablet or anything that has camera in it and start recording.

Put your head down and start working. It will take hours until you become a "natural". Of course, "natural" doesn't exist, but if you think it does, it's only an impediment in your head...

WHAT TO SAY AND NOT TO SAY ON FACEBOOK LIVES

As we talked in the Secret #4, if there's a crazy side of you, or if you have negativity in your life, keep it to yourself. Don't bring it on Facebook lives. Don't talk about your crazy girlfriend/boyfriend... No one cares. And, it's not related to your business.

But nevertheless, the content that's related to your market has to be polarizing and dramatic.

For example, if you say, "I will show you how to make money" that would not be polarizing at all and no one cares about a statement like that. But if you say: "Here's the #1 reason why you really suck at making money..." That probably will turn some people off, but... it will stop other people in their tracks and they will listen and they will like your message if it's helpful to them.

AWESOME CATCHY TITLES AND HEADLINES

The headlines have to be so irresistible that it makes people salivate. I don't care what headlines they are... Whether it's your blog, a Facebook post, or a Facebook live it's all about the words you use.

There's a great book that you probably need to get *The Words That Sell* by Richard Bayan that has these awesome key words that you can use anytime you create a headline. It's the thesaurus that matters almost always whenever you write. And headlines account for 80% of your sales.

As Gary Halbert (the best copywriter that ever lived) famously said: "More People Read Any Single Issue Of *The Enquirer* Than Have Read The Bible Since It Was First Printed!

Enquirer articles are superbly written. They are clear, concise, crisp and, all in all, the most easily understood articles of any publication.

And what do Enquirer writers excel at above all else? You guessed it -- HEADLINES. Their headlines are so powerful, they have so much grabbing power that, every week, people who have sworn they'll never again buy such a publication, are almost forced to purchase it in spite of themselves. ".

This is still true in 2020s and it will stay this way, because that's how our brains work.

Using the "power words" is the key.

For example, "Desperate Woman loses 277lbs With Amazing Diet Secret!" sounds better than "buy XYZ product to lose weight". And, "Doctors Prove That 2 out of 3 Women Can Have More Beautiful Skin In 14 Days" sounds better than "Find out how you can have a beautiful skin"...

"Power word" is like a zinger... It wakes you up! For example,

Just to help you out, you can use these power words:

- fast
- free
- easy
- proven
- guaranteed
- discover
- revealing
- how to
- save
- increase
- you

- your
- secret
- more
- at last
- winner
- hacks
- breakthrough
- 70% (any percent)
- $99.95 (currency)

(You can get more of these words in *The Words That Sell* book I mentioned earlier.)

If you are creating a headline for your ads, ad copy or your website copy. Try to use at least two or more power words.

Examples:

* * *

Discover how restaurants can save 50% on rent

* * *

Proven ways the construction companies can save 24% on uniforms

* * *

Revealing secrets that increased one waiter's pay 200%...

* * *

Download 100 awesome headlines in a PDF I created for you: http://geneadam.com/headlines

INTERVIEWS WITH OTHER PEOPLE

A quick way to get engagement is to invite somebody from the people in your industry and talk about what's going on in your field... This one thing gave me so many new followers. I didn't expect anything from it, but it worked like a charm. ☺

Qualify the people you do interviews with, don't just collaborate with anybody. Keep your standards high and produce high quality content. It will get you further down the road.

HONEST, VULNERABLE, AUTHENTIC STORIES, BEING REAL AND WHAT NOT TO BE VULNERABLE ABOUT

Your goal is to start telling dramatic stories that will evoke emotions. In the Secret #7 we talked about how dramatic you should get in your stories.

A rule of thumb I use to create dramatic stories:
1. Talk about something extremely bad that happened in your life (or people close to you)
2. And resolve it into a good lesson that people can learn from.

Stay away from talking about something extremely bad without a resolution or without at least a possible resolution in the future. It's how our brain works, we appreciate bad events that happened to somebody if we can learn something from it. But we won't appreciate bad events if we just talk about it without a point, because it's sad, gloomy and terrible. It's the transformation that makes us love those stories.

To help you be amazing on your Facebook Lives, you should be:
- Honest
- Vulnerable
- Authentic
- Real

And finally, tie the lesson of your story to what you do or what you sell, because people that relate to your story also have to be connected to your personal brand and your product so they buy in the future.

<u>Don't be vulnerable pointlessly</u>. If you cry on the camera and you don't have a lesson to teach that you've learned something from your mistakes, people will not open their wallets and buy your stuff… After all if you sound like a loser, there's no reason why they would want to buy anything from you.

On the other hand, if you cry about the fact that you lost your house, money, or your loved one but you learned from your mistakes, and it made you a bigger person and it made you realize that you have to change your life and start over, then you have a positive message! Of course, if you show amazing results you got after your transformation, it will do even better.

"3 SECRETS / IF ALL IT DID…" FB LIVE SCRIPT

The "3 secrets" script is one of the simplest scripts you can use when you make a Facebook Live. It works! I have learned this from my mentor Russell Brunson and then I simplified it. Russell used it for webinars. I use it for Facebook Lives.

It works like this:

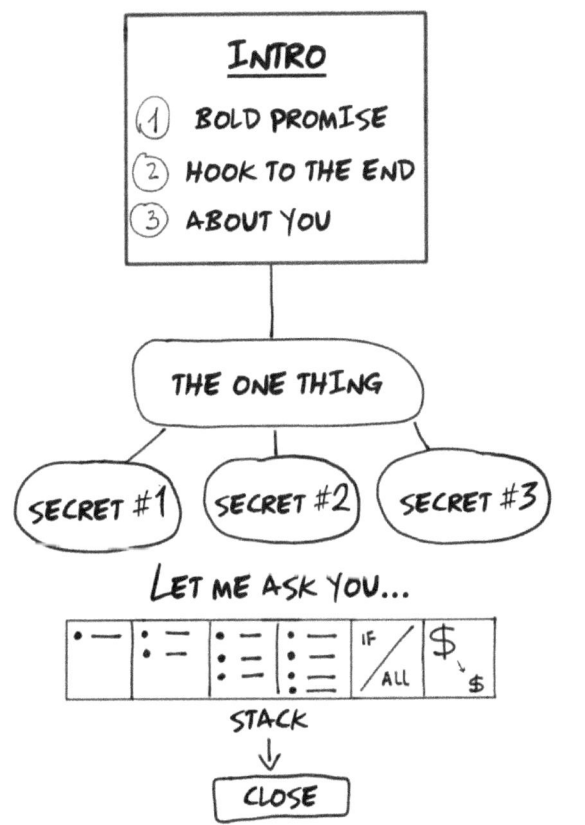

Before you create your Facebook Live, you need to know where you are going and have the end in mind. The "3 Secrets" script goes like this:
1. Come up with your big promise. For example, "How to X without Y" – "How to Get Traffic without Spending Money on Advertising"
2. Say something enticing so they stay till the end. For example, "If you stay with me until the end of this Facebook Live I'll give you a free cheat sheet how to X."
3. Remind them who you are. It doesn't hurt to tell them that you are an expert in X. This one is optional.
4. The one thing. Teach them about the main subject. It has to be related to your big promise.
5. "The one thing" will be divided into 3 secrets (3 sub-parts). Your secrets have to be real secrets, not known facts. For example, Secret #1: "How I got 1000 likes by posting one post on Facebook and how you can do the same or better".
6. Then you say: "Let me ask you a question…". This question takes the pressure off you and the listener. And you proceed to say almost anything… For example, "Let me ask you a question… Is this FB live beneficial to you?" or "Let me ask you a question, are you enjoy this Facebook Live? Is it helpful?"
7. Stack. Sell them an onion offer (Secret #8) and peel the layers of the offer. For example, you can say, "#1 You will get the training about X, #2 you also will get the booklet Y, #3 you will get access to our FB group",etc.

Every time you introduce another item in you offer, repeat each item from the beginning (#1 you will get X, #2 you will get Y, #3 you will get... etc). That's called a "stack". You should do it because people won't remember everything you are giving them, but if you repeat it they are more likely to buy it from you, because it has so many goodies in there.

By the way, if you don't have an offer it's fine. This step is optional, because you are not going to sell every single Facebook live.

8. "If all it did..." Then, ask them this question. "If all it did was ____ , would it be worth $____?". For example, "If all [whatever you are selling] brought you an extra $300 per month... Would it be worth it?"
9. Tell them what it's really worth (usually 10x) and drop the price by giving them an amazing deal.
10. "Close". You can do all kinds of closes in here. But if you are a beginner, it's enough if you just ask them for a "call to action". Example, "Interested? Just click on the link below the Facebook live and go to the checkout page..."

This script is only scratching the surface and it's oversimplified.

If you want to learn the full *Perfect Webinar Script* which I based the "3 Secrets" script on, go to the *Perfect Webinar* page and get it from Russell Brunson. He is amazing.

http://geneadam.com/perfect-webinar

ENGAGEMENT (TALK LIKE YOU ARE ON STAGE TALKING TO PEOPLE)

To trick the Facebook algorithm in an ethical way, talk through the camera to the people that are watching you and ask them to comment and like. For example, when they start watching you, tell them, "Say Hi if you see me", or "if you are watching the replay, comment replay", "what business are you in? comment in the chat" or "where are you from, comment below" or "what do you want me to cover next, please comment in the box below", etc. If you don't have enough people yet, ask the type of questions that people can answer after the live video is published.

Your goal is to come up with interesting questions that people are forced to engage with.

CONSISTENCY

All Facebook lives should be at least 15-30 minutes. If you are not getting the results you want on social media, go through this productivity checklist.

Download the PDF version of this checklist go to www.geneadam.com/productivity-checklist

ALWAYS CHECK YOUR POSITIONING AND TEST NEW IDEAS

Let's say that you are consistent and you put out great value. But don't forget about positioning yourself as an influencer and make sure that your profile is setup correctly, your message is consistent across all the platforms you are on and all the information besides the content is attractive. Adjust as you go. And always test new ideas. Markets change and your message could change slowly as you grow. Here's a quick checklist to make sure you look like an influencer:

- Is your profile set up correctly?
- Do you look trustworthy?
- Do you bring great value to your audience?
- Does your brand reflect the same values in your content and your profile?
- Are you consistent with information you put out in your niche?
- Are you building meaningful relationships?
- Are you putting your potential buyers in a group?
- Are you building an email list or Facebook Bot list?

Note: There's so much to do on social media. You can use it to be productive OR you can use it to waste time ⏳ If you can learn how to use social media the right way, you will attract great people into your life. Be the one that even YOU would follow. To scale your business, work on meaningful tasks every single day without any excuses.

Secret #11
How to Write Effective Posts

To write effective posts use "bad" stories as well as "good" stories… and turn it into something good in the end. i.e. so the reader can learn something in the end of your story.

Use the *Hook, Story, Transformation* formula whenever you can.

For short, *Hook* is basically a catchy headline. *Story* is the type of story that is emotional and move readers and break your reader's false beliefs. *Transformation* is what you learned from the story and the transformation has to happen in your listener's mind.

Here's how I would create a story.

1. I would start with a struggle or something hard that happened in your life (this opens you up in front of the viewers and builds trust. It makes you look like you are opening up and

telling them the truth. (It's totally NLP and very powerful. Don't use it for evil)
2. Teach them a lesson they can learn.
3. Show up as a leader and lead. Portray yourself as a leader by the end of the story) What does a leader do? Lead!

Don't end your story with the struggle. Because people will think you are a big mess.

Don't forget that that story has to be somehow connected to the products you sell. Also, you have to tell the stories to the right audience. Why?

Because confused people DO NOT BUY!

If you don't concentrate on the one thing that you offer, people won't buy anything.

Master one first and then move to other directions, but don't confuse your customers.

Here are some great pointers that will help you.

- Get personal, show personal aspects, be authentic.
- Use the word "YOU".
- Call to Action. When you post in groups – in the end of your posts say: "If you have any other questions comment below and I will answer…" or "if you have more questions I'll get back to you" – that shows people that you're not pitching. (if you are posting on your own timeline or group you don't have to do that)
- Show your audience that it's possible for them to achieve these results and that they can do it to. For example,

"Here are the 5 strategies that made me 5 figures last year"
- Lift them up - make them feel better after they read your posts
- Use happy pictures of you whenever you can. ☺ Your photo is your logo!
- If you have results add them to your content and use numbers whenever it's possible
- It's always nice when your clients talk well about you. use it into your content if you can.

CREATE CONTENT THAT GETS ATTENTION

Always create the content that gets attention, whether it's a Facebook live in your group or a Facebook post that you are posting in other groups.

Tai Lopez is giving away cars. Grant Cardone is giving away one million dollars on Facebook, Twitter and Instagram.

You don't have to do that, I get it, we are not as rich, but there are many other ways.

One thing you can give away to get attention is to give massive value for FREE. What can you give away today that can raise eye brows? There's always something out there that people need. You can spy on your competitors and see the FREE giveaways all over the place, but you have to come up with your own awesome value. That's what makes you, YOU.

If you have images of you that are unique, interesting, positive, smiling, funny, strange or weird but not too weird you can get attention by using those when you craft your Facebook posts.

The text should attract eye-balls too. Use emoji's in your headlines and posts.

Here is an example of a Facebook post I posted in other groups that got a bunch of likes and engagement and later brought me some new members to my group:

* * *

[HERE I PUT A CUTE PICTURE OF ME]

5 Things That YOU Are Probably Doing Wrong! 🍪 😤 💥 🔥 I learned these the hard way. I wish it was easier... But didn't do these myself until recently...

✅ #1. You are probably worrying about too many things BUT you are NOT creating your personal brand by creating videos and posting value content every single day...

✅ #2. Looking for the next new HOT technique... Stop looking. Start creating.

✅ #3. Not showing up in other FB groups. You should create/write content and publish it in other groups.

✅ #4. Buying traffic on FB... Don't buy traffic. Build audience for free first... when you start making 6 or 7 figures then buy ads.

✅ #5. You're not consistent enough... Get consistent. Show up every single day. And you will get amazing results... 1 FB live a day. 1 / Youtube video a day. Posting in other groups, at least 1 a day... etc

These are my 5 secrets rules I'm using every day :)

Comment and hit like if you like it :)
Gene Adam

* * *

SECTION FOUR:

HOW TO GET TRAFFIC, UNLIMITED FOLLOWERS, FANS AND BUYERS

In this section I will cover how to get unlimited traffic. Bold move, I know. But if you look at it from this new point of view everything will fall into place.

To get your audience. You need to:
Do 1 facebook live / day,
Or 1 youtube / day,
Or 1 podcast / day,
For 1 year and I guarantee you will have HUGE RESULTS.

Wait, why do you have to be on Facebook live to get customers? Because people start following you and listening to you. The word "traffic" is mostly unimportant and useless, but "engaged audience" is the name of the game. "Traffic" is blind. There is traffic happening here and there, but no one knows who those people are and probably they don't know you. So, if you buy traffic or pay for ads, it better be targeted. My recommendation is this:

> Don't buy traffic until you reach 6-7 figures.

This recommendation is supported by very big marketers in the industry and it's tested. There are exceptions, of course. But you can burn $10k ad budget within a couple of days and not get any results.

If you are starting, start with your personal brand and show up on Facebook Lives, videos and write posts.

Maybe you knew this, maybe not. I'm surprised how many people don't know this. Hopefully I started shifting your perception of "traffic" already.

In this section I will cover how to run your own Facebook Group, how to do Facebook Lives every day and how to stay consistent with it.

Also, I'll cover the 3X Multiplier Formula, which will help you show up everywhere. If you ask me what the quickest way to get exposure it would be this formula. Learn it and apply it.

Secret #12
How to Crush It With Facebook Groups

HOW TO RUN A SUCCESSFUL FACEBOOK GROUP

Here's a 7-steps that will help you create your own successful group and grow your audience:

1. Pick a relevant, keyword rich name. This will depend mainly on what your audience wants. (Secret #5)
2. Write your one-liner that solves a specific problem for your audience (one-liner is basically your "mission statement", but all in one sentence) . (Secret #6)
3. Figure out what offer you will be selling to them (Secret #8)
4. Create your story so you can connect with them (Secret #7)

5. Figure out what content you can teach that's engaging and wanted (Secret #9, #10 and #11)
6. Find the best similar groups to yours where your potential audience is
7. Post related valuable content in those groups. 2-3 posts a day per group

Some steps have references to other secrets from this book so if you don't know what it means - look it up and I'm sure it will fall into place and create your group without a problem.

The step 6 and 7 will help you get unlimited leads in your Facebook group for free. Let me show you how.

HOW TO ETHICALLY STEAL AUDIENCE FROM OTHER GROUPS

Just start searching for groups where your perfect audience is. Choose between 3-5 groups that have at least 5000 people and post there daily. Post in at least one of them by adding pure value. You content should educate, and therefore attract those who want to learn more about you.

I went over how to create posts in the Secret #11.

> You have to show up every day and post 3 pieces of content in each group.

To become an influencer faster post every day, not every other day!

If you could just learn this one thing from the whole book and actually apply it, I did my job. If you post in other niche related groups for the next 90 days consistently most likely you'll have a MAJOR breakthrough!

If you can do 10 groups x 3, which is 30 posts a day, you'll get an avalanche of people coming to check you out and some of them will start joining your group.

Just imagine people flooding your wall, friend requesting you and joining your group on autopilot, without you running after them and begging them to become friends…

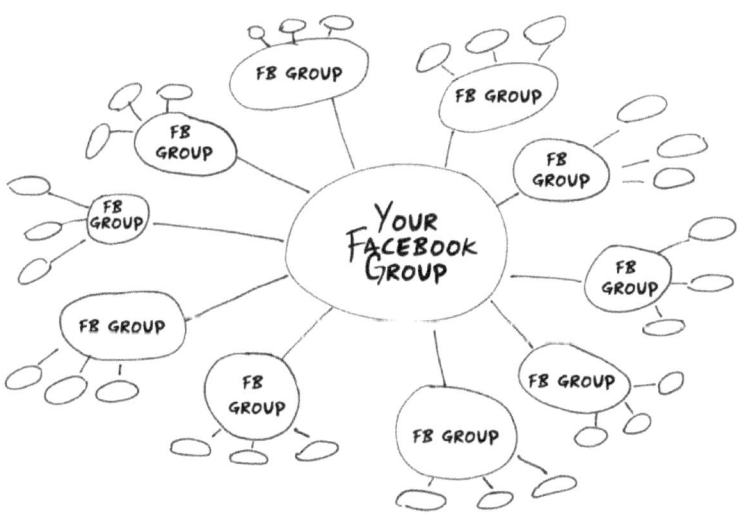

Here are a few rules you need to know about posting in groups:

1. No duplicate posts. All of your posts MUST be unique
2. The post should provide MASSIVE value
3. All posts should be posted at least 20 minutes apart
4. No links. Most groups don't allow you to post links. But no one can stop you from putting VALUE content.

In fact, group owners love you when you post value content and your posts get likes, comments and shares, because it grows their groups too.

And when your posts are all over the place, some people will want to find out more about you. They'll go to your profile and click on your pictures and links there. Of course, then, when they click on your links you can opt them in, send them to your group and take them through your buying process…

And voila! You got unlimited traffic for free, except that you have to put some hours in…But the good news it works!

By the way, if 30 posts a day are too many to start with, just start with 1 group and go up to 10, that way you can 10x your results!

HOW TO SPREAD LIKE A VIRUS BEYOND FACEBOOK GROUPS

So let's say that you do 30 posts x 10 groups and you get 300 posts a day. Maybe you hire a team that does it for you or maybe you are a workaholic like me. And then you say, how do I expand? You have to take this Facebook group model and instead of showing up in Facebook groups you need to replace it with what that platform has to offer. So let's say we decided to do podcasts. Here's how it would work with podcasts:

Become friends with podcasters and ask them if you could be a guest on their show. In the end of the podcast there is always a line the podcaster says: "So, how can they find you?"

This is where you send them to a link to your Facebook group or your lead magnet.

Here is what you can do with doing interviews on other people's YouTube channels:

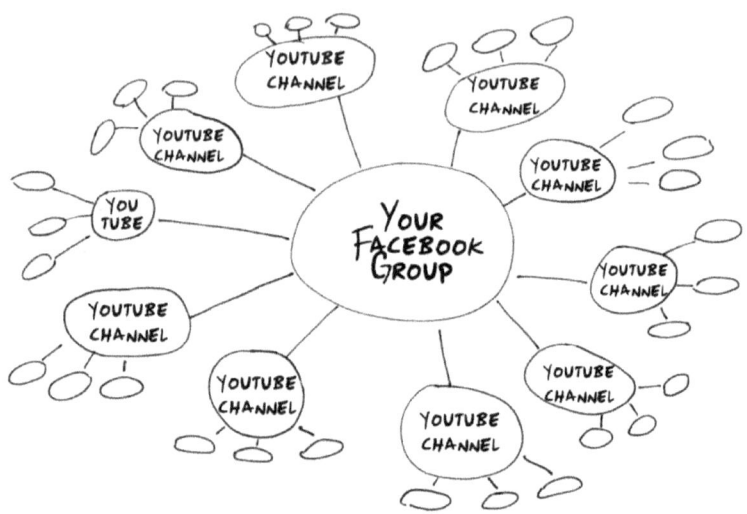

Contact Youtubers that have a lot of channel subscriptions already and ask them to be a guest on their channel. In the end when they say "How can they learn more about you", send them to your Facebook group.

And finally, if that's not advanced enough and you are already doing this, then go back to the Secret #2 and get on all of the platforms and I'll see you on top! 😊

GET REAL PROSPECTS FROM OTHER FACEBOOK GROUPS

So how do you get the REAL PROSPECTS from a Facebook Group for free?

You can do that by posting in Facebook Groups.

Step 1. Find 3-5 Facebook groups in your niche with at least 20,000 people in them and high engagement.

Step 2. Write a post in each group once a day. Great attention-grabbing headline is a must. Add emoticons.

Step 3. You can cover almost anything that is related in your niche, anything that provides amazing value and gets a lot of likes and a lot of comments. Tell stories. Stories are great. Write a moral of the story. I recommend writing posts where you had a personal transformation. You learned something. Tell experiences how you dealt with problems and how you solved them. Or, you can write the type of stories that talk about what you are currently working on.

Step 4. Before posting, add a smiling photo of you or something attention grabbing (high quality).

When you have results increase the amount of Facebook Groups to 10 (step 1) and amount of posts to 3 (step 2). That will help you grow faster.

So here's an example of a Facebook post that got me several hundreds of likes:

* * *

Why I quit my 💰$26K e-commerce biz and why I started doing affiliate marketing… and why I went with ClickFunnels.

I know, I know... Who in their sober mind would quit $26K a month biz? But my supplier was an a**hole and the stress wasn't worth it...

Here's my two cents on it... Sometimes you can snatch a lot of money quick and you could be very unhappy (it doesn't have to be that way BTW) or you can enjoy the ride and give it ALL YOU GOT. You can give all the love of you to your business... and make a little bit less $...

I wasn't sleeping at night because I worked in the biz like a headless chicken...

Why wasn't I sleeping? Because I was scared... I was scared that something wrong will happen... There was something that could go wrong... There was always something with the web site, or the advertising campaign or supplier...

And it sure did go wrong....

In the mean time, I've invested $120,000 in advertising, and I became the #1 seller of this product... and we made $26K per month... crazy... I know...

But then my jealous supplier... decided to cut everybody off...

Because we were making so much money, the dude who made the main product we were selling, got us on the call...

And here we were waiting in anticipation... There was something important he wanted to talk about...

He said: "We decided to stop allowing our retailers advertise our product on major sites, i.e. Google, Amazon, etc "... "We can sell our product by ourselves to the customers that are within our reach", he slowly said, "and you can't advertise with our name on it"

And I was like..... "what????????"...."seriously????" We can't advertise your brand name? It's like if I sell NIKE shoes I can't make ads that advertise "NIKE shoes"? They said: "Yep. Our brand name can't be on the ads"... It's like saying you can only advertising that you are just selling "shoes"...

After I've spent $120,000 on advertising... are you telling me that now you want to sell your product yourself???? WTH?

Yep, that's why I was out. That really hit me... I quit... If you can decide not to have a boss - that's the best thing you can do for yourself...

If you have a supplier with a trademark, they can tell you "goodbye" anytime... Just like what I experienced.

Affiliate biz I am in, is different... I sold a $1000 course - they loved me... they paid 40% - $400... I sold a $97/month Click Funnels account and they pay me 40% - that's about $38/month. I love it... They love me... I advertise I still got my customers' emails and contacts... That's the way it should be... I can walk away with my following... and sell my people whatever I like.. They are my people and I take them with me... They respect me.... No problem...

If you ask me... I don't want to sell e-commerce, unless I'm the inventor and the trademark owner...

I'd rather be a residual affiliate for Russell Brunson that makes $38/month per person... If I sell just 30 people I can get around $1200 every single month... And then the next month if I get another 30 people I'll get $2400 and then the next month I'll get $3600 and every month it will snowball from there... It's a dream business for me and I can give all I got for something I love... I love affiliate marketing...

So this is why I quit the 26K/month of injustice... jealousy... just because I was the best seller of the product. I suffered the most...

The moral is do what you love on your own terms...

I chose Click Funnels. And I already made over $700 in sales with Click Funnels...

To summarize:
1. Be your own boss - have your own terms 😎
2. Own your own product
3. Have your own audience
4. It's better to make less in the beginning and have a snowball income coming later. It will come rolling in exponentially...

Sincerely,
Gene Adam 🖤

p.s. I hope this inspires some people here...

[AND I POSTED A NICE PICTURE OF ME]

* * *

Next, don't forget to point the link in your bio and profile image to your Facebook group as I mentioned in the Secret #4.

You want all the traffic that comes to your Facebook profile join your group.

Note: Beware. While text posts with pictures are fine, you can't post any links, videos or lives in those groups, because the owners usually don't like it. If it's considered self-promotion, they'll block you and then you are out. Check the rules of those groups.

Secret #13
Do 1 Facebook Live Every Day

BUT I GOT NO TIME!

All of the mentors I have ever had one thing in common. They all showed up every day like clockwork.

But most small entrepreneurs come up to me and say, "Gene, I need more sales and I need to scale my business, can we schedule a meeting?"

"When do you want to start?", I ask them.

They usually say something similar to this, "On Monday I have to take care of my family, on Tuesday I got a lunch with my buddies and in the afternoon I'm going to a bachelor party, so I'm going to be busy, on Wednesday I'm travelling to see my cousin, we always hang out together once a week, I have to catch up with my family, you know? On Thursday evening my friend has a birthday party. And on Friday I got meetings with my clients on the phone and then I got to create some funnels."

"What about Saturday?"

"Oh no, I don't want to work on Saturdays, I got to clean up the house, cut the grass, and do some errands around the house. And, I need to see my wife and kids. "

"And How about Sunday?", I asked.

"Sunday we have a football game, I gotta see this game, this one is a VERY important game this season."

Really? A very important game??? Are you serious? So, if you are not going to give up a very important game to change your life, then I can't help you. I'm done. If you are comfortable where you are and you won't hustle, your life will NOT change.

You see the football game is played by someone else, not by you so it might change the life of a football player, but not your life.

Back in the 80s, when I was around 10-year-old, I once told my dad, "Dad, I think that human beings consist of 2 kinds of people: 'Watchers' and 'Doers'.. 'Watchers' watch successful people on TV, while the successful people simply DO things and live their life…" I still don't know how a 10-year-old kid could come up with such a brilliant and profound idea. LOL.

Don't misread me. I'm not bashing football or your favorite team. If you enjoy it, it's all good. I enjoy it too. But what I am saying is that you need to put YOURSELF before your favorite football team. When your life is set and you are where you want to be, then no problem, you can watch the football day and night and I'll be happy for you. But if your life is unbearable, is it what you gonna do?

If you want to stay a small entrepreneur, fine, stay small, but don't complain you don't have enough leads and sales, and don't ask to scale your business. YOU are your worst enemy. And also, YOU are your true savior. If you want to learn more about how you are possibly your own enemy then there's an awesome book called *The Ego Is Your Enemy* by Ryan Holiday. I also didn't want to admit I was my own enemy, but I was wrong and that's why I recommend this book to you.

So <u>if you want to grow and become a successful entrepreneur</u> you need to reverse your world. You need to buy some time for YOURSELF and put everything else on hold. The exception to the rule would be your health and your family, but even your family has to start respecting your working hours. If you worked in a restaurant, your Mom and Dad couldn't call you anyway, could they? Unless it's an emergency. So why would your small business suffer from being available anytime?

The same thing applies to your phone. If you are at work you can't pick up your phone and talk to your friends and you can't get on the Facebook either. So, put your phone away. And voila, now you should have a few hours available to do Facebook lives.

CONSISTENCY

So now that we cleared up some of your time, let's talk about the consistency. You need to do Facebook Lives every single day. No excuses.

So, if a Facebook Live lasts only 15 minutes, can you do it every single day? Look, if you got 1440 minutes available per day and even if you sleep and eat 12 hours per day, you still got 720 minutes left. Do you think you could get on the camera and talk for a little bit? You probably can.

If you still can't, Your WHY is probably not bigger than your fears.

Refer to Secret #4. If you already GOT the big why, then 99% of you will answer 'yes'.

To scale your business, work on meaningful tasks every single day without any excuses.

The example tasks that will help you scale your business:
- 1 facebook live / day
- 1 youtube / day
- 1 podcast / day

etc…

In 1 single day it will seem like nothing is happening. It will seem as you are banging your head against the wall. No improvement whatsoever. And it's totally normal. Then 1 person will pop up out of nowhere. Then 2..3..4.. And then they will come in droves. But you need to continue on giving them amazing FREE value, break their false beliefs (Secret #4), and in 1 year it will accumulate and turn into HUGE RESULTS.

There's a great book *The Compound Effect* by Darren Hardy that talks about small little steps that compound into one BIG change. I've watched Neil Patel adding 1 blog a day for years, that resulted into one of the biggest blogs on the internet. I've watched Ben Settle writing one email a day that made him the best email copywriter in the world. I've watched iJustine making 1 video a day on YouTube that made her one of the most watched people on Youtube. She's got almost 5 million subscribers and some of her videos get 10 million views! If you just stick to one video per day in your niche… The sky is your limit.

HOW TO STAY EFFECTIVE

If you are not getting the results you want on social media, go through this productivity checklist.

Download the PDF version of this checklist go to
www.geneadam.com/productivity-checklist

Answer these questions every time you create your content.

* * *

SECTION #1 - **Make sure you get at least 1 YES**
Did you post at least 1 FB live today?
Did you post at least 1 YouTube Video today?
Did you post at least 1 Podcast today?
Did you post at least 1 Long FB Post today?

SECTION #2 - **YES to all answers**
Did you post at least 3 posts in OTHER groups today?
Did any of those posts make at least 3-5 likes?
Did you make a few new connections today?

SECTION #3 - **at least 3 YES'es**
Did you engage in your own group today?
Did you engage on your wall today?
Did you give A LOT OF VALUE to others today in some other way?

Don't forget to grow your followers on Facebook. You need to have at least 700+ people following you, so people trust your persona. If you don't, then make new friends in the Facebook groups that are related to your niche.

There is one secret that can get you a lot of followers quick. You can start using it right away. Open the post that is directly related to your niche. And click on everyone who liked this post. Send them a friend request and some of them will add you and start following you.

Secret #14
How to Show Up Everywhere - 3X Content Multiplier

I learned this formula from Peng Joon. It's called 3x content multiplier formula. The way it works is that you create just one video but then you repurpose it on 3 platforms: Facebook, Youtube, Instagram. You do it all in different times a few months apart so it's always looks unique. If you got a team to help you, you can get on podcasts, blogs and other places.

And then, you transcribe it and use the text for Facebook long posts, Instagram quotes, and even your blog. Now that was the content only from one video.

But the best secret I learned from Peng Joon was that you have to do it in batches. You need to create 120 videos all at once which will last for a few months. So you don't have to do the repetitive tasks hundreds of times...

How effective is it when you publish 120 videos every single day on those platforms? Almost not effective at all. 95% won't take off. But the 5% that will take off will be so effective that you will be everywhere. You'll be on the top of everyone's timeline and you'll get a lot of exposure. Just this one secret can make you the top influencer! It is the make it or break it material.

So here's the golden content formula that you should implement right away in your business, if you are not doing it yet.

3X CONTENT MULTIPLIER FORMULA

Step 1. Come up with 120 topics.
Step 2. Spend 3 days shooting 120 videos.
Step 3. Edit Videos
Step 4. Organize the content and post dates in Excel Sheet
Step 5. Post 1 video per day on Facebook as a "Video".
Step 6. Post 1 quote a day on Instagram
Step 7. Schedule the same video to show up two months later on YouTube and Instagram
Step 8. Transcribe the video content and edit the text for a long Facebook post and schedule it

Step 9. (optional) Create a blog post from the step 8.

Step X. (optional) Think about how to show up in other places. i.e. you can get the audio track out of the video and create a podcast...

SECTION FIVE:
CREATING YOUR FUNNEL, BONUSES AND UPSELLS

So in the first section of the book we went over how influencers stay influencers by being everywhere:

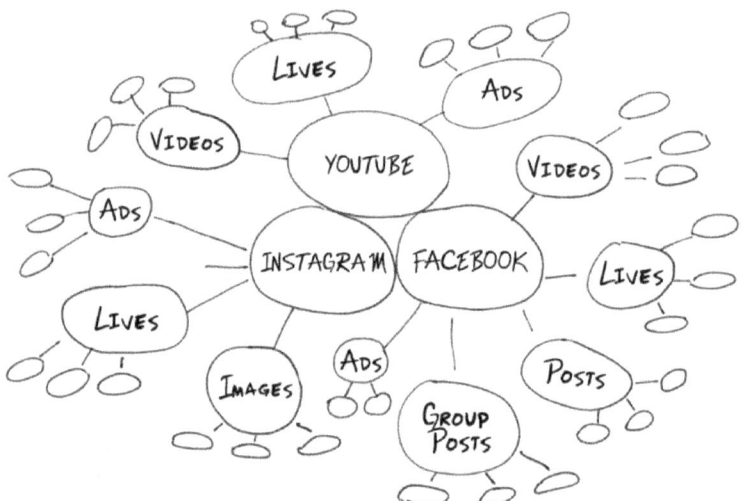

And then, we went over the 5 cores: YOU, THEM, PROBLEM, STORY, SELLING in the 2nd section.

Then we covered how you can create your content and how to get unlimited followers and buyers to your Facebook page.

And now I want to talk about the Facebook funnel and automation.

Secret #15
Facebook Profile Funnel

Facebook profile funnel (F.P.F.) is very crucial to your influencer success on Facebook. Your main picture in your profile is a very expensive real estate, so you should leverage in your favor. When somebody looks you up on Facebook and opens up you profile, what do they see? The first picture they see is your HUGE profile background picture. What do you have in there?

Is that a quote? Meh, no one cares about the quotes. And if they do they don't associate you with an influencer just because you put a quote of Einstein.

Is that an ocean without writing? Okay, not bad. The life of an entrepreneur after they succeed might have an element of a vacation. But still no!

Is that a smiling picture of you? Ok, better. So, you got some personality going on. But still no. It could be more effective.

You need to write a message on your profile background image to your potential customer with an offer. Let's say you are coaching course creators. Say, "Hey course creators! Get a free cheat sheet that will explode your audience and get you a bunch of sales!"

And don't forget to draw a button that makes them to take action. Even though the button is technically not a real button, but it looks like a button so people will click on it.

When you click on the profile background image it actually opens up the description box on the left and that is where you can put some text and links! And they are clickable links! YES! That's exactly what we need!

Wow! Looking great!

So I usually recommend to have 2 links. One link should lead to your opt-in funnel and the second link can ask them to join your group. Or if you don't have an offer yet, ask them just to join your group.

In the text you can write your text description like this:

* * *

Go To www.yourdomain.com/cheatsheet to get your FREE cheat sheet and explode your business with these awesome hacks…

Come Join me In my Awesome FREE Facebook Group and Hangout with Course Creators just Like You! www.geneadam.com/group

* * *

Some people will click, some people won't but if your offer is SO compelling many will take you up on your offer.

So now you got your Facebook profile working for you on autopilot. It guides people to your normal funnel with opt-in box and gives them a cheat sheet or some kind of PDF, or even a physical book. That's your job to figure out what's needed in your niche.

If you are not using this method right now, please stop everything and create your profile background image now. Find a nice-looking background and put an actionable headline on it. Create a button. Write the description with your links and send them to your opt-in page. After they sign up and get the freebie you can start selling them your products.

So, this is it for your Facebook profile funnel, now you need to create opt-in funnel. You can do this with Clickfunnels. If you don't have it get a free trial here: www.geneadam.com/cf

I won't be covering how to create the actual pages in this book, but if you need your funnel created for you or if you don't know where to start, we might be able to help you. Go to the next chapter to find out more and we might be able to design a funnel for you. The funnel is worth at least $1000! If you qualify, it's yours free.

BONUSES

Create a lot of bonuses for people (3 to 5 bonuses) no matter what you sell. Just shower people with bonuses. Find anything that they might need and give it to them. It could be:
- Video trainings, Web classes, Mini courses
- Templates
- Cheatsheets, Worksheets or Checklists
- E-books or PDFs
- Physical Books or Brochures

- Audio Interviews (or video)
- Photoshop Design Files
- Ipads or any electronic item (if the budget allows)
- T-shirts, Flashlights
- Cars (yes, some big influencers give away cars)

Also you can create anything that can save them time and money. Your bonuses must stand out. Make it such a no brainer for people that they don't have a choice but buy your stuff.

As my mentor says create bonuses as good as, or better than the products you sell. Make them so desirable that they can't say no.

UPSELLS

Always have upsells. 90% of people don't have upsells and that's why they are poor. The money is in the backend. Don't concentrate on low ticket items, but on what comes next! You can sell a $37 product and ask if they also want a $199 training and or a $497 1-on-1 coaching.

MacDonald's doesn't make any money if you buy a cheeseburger. When they ask, "Would you like fries with that?" Cha-ching! They made $1.50. "Would you like a drink with that?" Cha-ching! They just made another $1.50. "Do you want to upgrade to our large combo deal?, it's only $1 more?". Yep! Create. Upsells. Now.

Want a Highly Converting Funnel Done-For-You for FREE? (Value:$1000)

ONE-TIME OFFER

To overdeliver I'm going to do something completely CRAZY for you. I'm going to design a custom high converting web funnel for your business (worth $1000) for absolutely FREE. This is such a no brainer offer that you'd be silly not to take it.

My amazing team will help you create a custom funnel specifically to suit your business.

With this funnel you can:
1. Build your list and follow up with them
2. Convert lookie-loos into buyers
3. Sell them your coaching, courses, books, services and products
4. Upsell your list again and again on new products you will have in the future

Because of many entrepreneurs would like to get this offer, I cannot possibly take on hundreds of these funnels, it would be physically impossible for me and my team to help you all. So, I put a requirement in place. You will need to be qualified for this offer. Below are the requirements.

By the way, if you don't qualify for the free offer you still can contact us and depending on the load, you still might be able to hire our team.

HOW TO QUALIFY FOR THE FREE FUNNEL

So here are the requirements to get this free offer.

1. You must have a clear idea of what you are going to sell. If you are already selling something – great. If not, make sure that you are ready with your plan.

2. Even though we will create a custom funnel for you, you still have to provide us with your content: graphics and copy. Without your content the funnel will not work.

3. This offer is only for entrepreneurs that don't have a Clickfunnels account yet. You'll have to sign up with my team, and they will walk you through the process and help you open the account with Clickfunnels. Later the funnel will be created in the same account.

4. We use only Clickfunnels software to create funnels for the speed of implementation purposes and in order for

you to continue having your funnel, you need to maintain your Clickfunnels membership (at the moment of writing it's $97/month).

5. We can only build one funnel per customer.

If you qualify for the free offer, please go to: www.geneadam.com/funnel

Conclusion

Congratulations, you got to the last part of this book. Did you know that most people never reach the end? You are a really dedicated person. Kudos to you! 😍

Growing your influence is the best thing you can do to have unlimited customers.

So here's what we have done:
1. We figured out why influencers are getting so damn rich
2. How influencers get results
3. Influencers grow audiences. One of the practical ways to do it is to join many like-minded people to your FB group
4. Learned how to build YOU as an influencer
5. Learned how to find THEM – your audience
6. Learned how to write your STORY
7. Learned how to SELL without selling
8. Then we went over the Facebook Profile Funnel

Sweet. That's a lot of information to get you started and get amazing results. Use this book as a bible and come back to it. You'll find a lot of hidden things in this book if you read it twicc. 😁

Depending on the type of business you are in, one strategy can work better than the other. So, test it and choose the strategy that works best for you and then 10x it.

WHAT'S NEXT?

Scale. Expand into different platforms. Find mentors that can get you there faster than if you were to do it by yourself.

> In fact, get my **Influencer Secrets** course that will teach you how to become an influencer 10 times faster! (Just in few months)
> Get it here: www.geneadam.com/influencer

WHAT'S BEYOND A SUCCESSFUL INFLUENCER?

The most important part what many entrepreneurs forget is that it's not about looking good. It is not about becoming a fake persona. It's not about being a flashy influencer. It's not about cute and shiny pictures of you. If you got nothing to offer except that, then you failed! You still can have all the nice pictures of your cars, houses and vacations, but it shouldn't be the main course. It should be the side dish. Or, maybe just a dessert. But definitely not the main course! The main course should be the value you provide to the world – never forget that.

So what's the end goal of being an influencer?

Do you remember your WHY that we talked about in the beginning of the book? Well this is what it's all about. It's about changing the lives around you and making the world a better place. You can make an impact in the world. Start changing the world by donating 10% of your earnings to the cause that you care about the most. As my mentor once said you can donate money at any stage. When you are rich or broke. 10% of $100,000 is $10,000. 10% of $10 is $1.

And on this note I want to say this.

I love you guys. I support you guys. Check out my site http://www.geneadam.com/

I'd love to work with you to try to make this world a better place.

Thank you for entrusting me with your time and reading this book.

😊

Truly Yours,
Gene Adam
Your Influencer Expert

References

Abagnale, Frank with Stan Redding. *Catch me if you can: The True Story of a Real Fake.* Broadway Books. 2000.

Bayan, Richard. *Words that Sell: More than 6000 Entries to Help You Promote Your Products, Services, and Ideas.* 2006

Brunson, Russell. *Expert Secrets.* Morgan J. Publishing 2015.

Cardone, Grant. *The 10X Rule: The Only Difference Between Success and Failure.* 2011.

Ezarik, iJustine. *I, Justine: An Analog Memoir.* 2015.

Halbert, Gary. *The Boron Letters.* 1986.

Hardy, Darren. *The Compound Effect.* 2012

Jeffreys, Susan. *Feel The Fear and Do it Anyway.* 1998.

Holiday, Ryan. *The Ego Is Your Enemy.* 2016.

Kim, W. Chan and Renee Mauborgne. *Blue Ocean Strategy.* Harvard Business Review Press. 2005.

Miller, Donald. *Building a StoryBrand: Clarify Your Message So Customers Will Listen.* 2017.

Nassim, Taleb. *Black Swan: The Impact of the Highly Improbable.* 2010.

Vaynerchuk, Gary. *Crush It!: Why NOW Is the Time to Cash In on Your Passion.* 2009.
Vaynerchuk, Gary. *Crushing It!: How Great Entrepreneurs Build Their Business and Influence-and How You Can, Too* 2018.

What is a funnel?

A funnel is the set of steps a visitor needs to go through before they reach the checkout page. In other words, It's a combination of pages that leads people to the "BUY" button…

Why funnels are better than normal websites?

Because funnels convert 10X better (or more) than websites.

Who would benefit from funnels?

This could be anyone, including entrepreneurs, authors, local business owners, coaches, consultants, health and wellness providers, real estate professionals, sales people, online business owners… It doesn't matter what market you are in. It's a method.

Want to get your own funnel?

My mentor Russell Brunson has an awesome class about funnels.

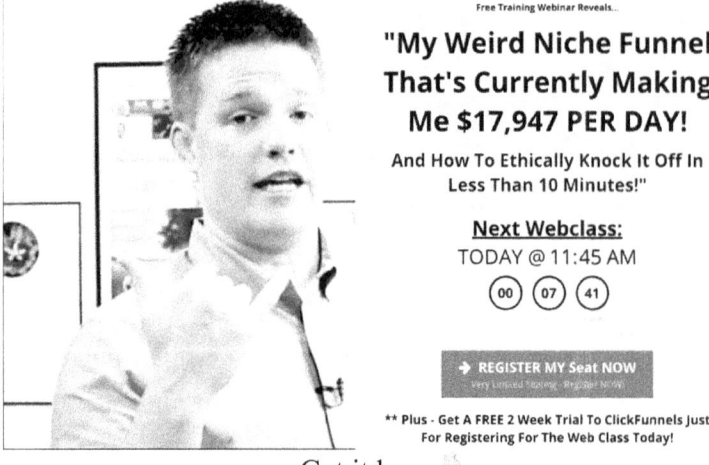

Get it here

www.geneadam.com/webtraining

www.ingramcontent.com/pod-product-compliance
Lightning Source LLC
Chambersburg PA
CBHW071024240526
45469CB00006BD/2074